# THE THIRD CULTURE TEEN

D1694939

# THE THIRD CULTURE TEEN:

## IN BETWEEN CULTURES, IN BETWEEN LIFE STAGES

JIWON LEE

NEW DEGREE PRESS

COPYRIGHT © 2020 JIWON LEE

*All rights reserved.*

THE THIRD CULTURE TEEN:

*In Between Cultures, In Between Life Stages*

| ISBN | | |
|---|---|---|
| | 978-1-64137-945-8 | *Paperback* |
| | 978-1-64137-754-6 | *Kindle Ebook* |
| | 978-1-64137-755-3 | *Ebook* |

*This book is dedicated to my parents, whom I cannot thank enough for raising me to be the Third Culture Kid I am today.*

# CONTENTS

———

# INTRODUCTION

———

"Where are you from?"

*This* question always made small talk impossible for me. At parties, at club events, in classrooms, or in a line at a concert—it has always been the same.

But above all other difficult small talk I've engaged in, the one I remember most clearly was on the lawn on the first night of college orientation.

Nobody knew each other. We were all sharing free In-N-Out from the school and desperately trying to socialize and make friends. I remember this one girl I was sharing the same picnic blanket with.

The August breeze felt perfect. The In-N-Out tasted great. And we were both smiling at each other. She asked my name. I asked hers. This was looking amazing. I was going to make my new best friend.

And *that* was the question she asked me next.

It felt like a ticking bomb went off. My heart began to feel stuffy and I could almost feel sweat trickling down my forehead. She kept looking at me with such innocent eyes. Can I blame her? It's the perfect conversation starter. I could have answered *Los Angeles, New York, or Beijing*—anywhere I could proudly claim I belong to. It would have led to a friendly response by default.

*Oh, I've been there. Oh, I have a cousin there. Oh, I've heard of there.*

Before I finally decided on a coherent answer, another girl next to me answered first.

"Oh, I'm from Pasadena."

"Wait, no way! My best friend's from Pasadena. Do you happen to know so-and-so high school?"

I remember not being able to say anything afterward. I knew that diving into the middle of that conversation and explaining the complicated international list of cities I have lived in was not going to elicit the same response. Maybe a polite "that's cool," but nothing more than that. It almost felt like my *one chance* to make friends in college completely died.

I was totally unrelatable.

If my story sounds even remotely familiar, then you just might be a Third Culture Kid—or a TCK for short.

The classic academic definition of a Third Culture Kid is as follows:

*A person who has spent a significant part of [their] developmental years outside the parents' culture. The TCK builds relationships to all of the cultures, while not having full ownership in any. Although elements from each culture are assimilated into the TCK's life experience, a sense of belonging is in relationship to others of similar background.*[1]

You might have heard the term before in your life, or you might not have. In my case, I have heard the term numerous times during my many years in international schools. At some point, after years of repeated special guest lectures on TCKs, it became a kind of joke in our school. Whenever a kid acted weirdly or did not understand common references, we would laugh and call them a TCK.

Only when I arrived in college did the term TCK hit me. Back in my safe community of fellow expatriates, explaining the long list of places we had lived in was the norm: Kuala Lumpur, Malaysia for four years, then Qingdao, China, for five, and a brief couple of years in Seoul, Korea. . . Now that I was in college, surrounded by non-expats—including, in fact, kids who were born and raised in the same town their whole lives—I realized just how *different* I was from everybody else. I was never just from "Wisconsin" or "the Bay Area." But

---

1    David C. Pollock, Ruth E. Van Reken, and Michael V. Pollock, *Third Culture Kids: Growing Up Among Worlds* (Boston: Nicholas Brealey Publishing, 2010), 15.

I could not dare explain it further because nobody would understand me.

Amid my semester of identity crises, I couldn't help but be reminded of the many successful TCKs I've learned about in TCK seminar from high school. Barack Obama was half Kenyan and spent his childhood years in Jakarta, Indonesia.[2] Freddie Mercury spent his childhood years in Zanzibar, India, then later in the UK.[3] Audrey Hepburn was born in Belgium and moved between Brussels, Arnhem, the Hague, and London, eventually settling in the UK in her later life.[4] Even beyond those famous figures, you can easily find thousands of successful adults who have grown up in different countries throughout their lives. I just could not wrap my head around how these successful adult TCK came to be. I hardly had the guts to introduce where I'm from to my college friends. How did these people reconcile their numerous cultural identities, manage to assimilate into a society where being an expat is not necessarily the norm, and even beyond that, use their background to their advantage?

That's when it struck me: the big gap between being a Third Culture Kid and being an *Adult* Third Culture Kid.

2   *Encyclopædia Britannica*, s.v. "Barack Obama," by Jeff Wallenfeldt and David Mendell, last modified February 12, 2020.

3   *Encyclopædia Britannica*, s.v. "Freddie Mercury," by The Editors of Encyclopaedia Britannica, last modified March 19, 2020.

4   *Encyclopædia Britannica*, s.v. "Audrey Hepburn," by The Editors of Encyclopaedia Britannica, last modified May 4, 2020.

A certain period exists when you are merely a *Third Culture Teen* (TCT). You are no longer a Third Culture "Kid" when you leave the comforts of your family and home of fellow expats. Yet, you feel so uncertain about your own identity that you can't quite call yourself an "Adult" Third Culture Kid.

Along my journey of writing and preparing for this book, I have had conversations with numerous teenage TCKs and adult TCKs who actually struggled with the same questions I had so much trouble with just last year. I thought I was the only one asking all these questions about where I am from and what community of people I belong to, the languages and cultures I feel comfortable with, and whether I should even feel that way. But all Third Culture Teens struggled with the same questions and overcame their hardships in their own ways.

This was so unimaginably encouraging for me, and I so very wish that I had the opportunity to speak with fellow Third Culture Kids last year when I hit the peak of my identity crisis.

So here it is, a book I wish I had in my freshman year of college.

This book is dedicated to all my fellow Third Culture Teens who are struggling to find a place in this world.

It includes an overview of what a Third Culture Kid is, and how it has an identity of its own. I have also included stories of the numerous Third Culture Kids I have interviewed and their wise tips on what helped them overcome their identity crises, including stories of how they used their Third Culture Kid identity to their advantage in their lives.

Threading these different stories together is my own reflection on growing up and transitioning between Korea, Malaysia, China, and the United States, which I hope you can relate to and use as an opportunity to reflect back upon your life as well.

Being an expat means a life of journeying—not only a physical journey around the world but a psychological one within yourself.

One clear answer to "where are you from?" will never exist (as you will find out in this book).

But I hope this book can be a guide in your continued journey of identity.

# PART 1:

# THE THIRD CULTURE KID & THE THIRD CULTURE TEEN

# CHAPTER 1:

# THE TCK & ITS VARIATIONS

———

*"I think somehow trying to understand my own story puts language on what happened."*

— RUTH VAN REKEN

Sitting in a seminar room surrounded by my high school classmates, I learned the term "Third Culture Kid" for the first time. The old projector wheezed as the teacher showed us a PowerPoint filled with graphs and terms we could not care less about. At our international school, the practice of all the seniors learning about the term "Third Culture Kid" was standard. We talked about ways to get through college as a TCK and memorized terms with similar definitions, including "global nomad," coined by researcher Norma McCaig, or simply just an "expat"—a person living outside their home country.

At the time, "TCK" meant nothing to me or my classmates. All we wanted to do was get out of that stuffy seminar room already and go eat lunch. I'm sure a lot of other TCKs from international schools went through the same experience—PowerPoints, group exercises, and guest lecturers—all telling you who you are and labeling you with a term you don't identify with. The truth is back when I was a high school student surrounded by other TCKs, I didn't see a reason to label ourselves or make a big deal out of our pasts. Why did I need this special term when everybody else came from a similar background?

Only when I went to college did I realize that I was in desperate need of a specific word to describe myself. I felt a constant need to shorten the statement "I was born in Korea, but lived in Malaysia for three years, then moved to China and lived there for a couple of years, and my family still lives in China, so my home is in China" whenever someone asked me where I am from.

During my second semester of college, I started researching the term "TCK" on my own. I was surrounded by monocultural kids who could not relate to my past and my struggles. Suddenly the word in itself made me feel at home—wherever that is supposed to be. I felt comforted that I was not alone in feeling restless and disconnected from the world around me and that an entire community of TCKs all across the globe could understand how I feel.

The word TCK, hence, has tremendous meaning to me now—yet its definition is not well-known by many people, including TCKs themselves.

In this chapter, I will be reviewing the established definitions and studies on the word TCK and its variations in hopes that these terms can help you clarify your identity as they did for me.

## A BRIEF HISTORY OF "TCK"

The term "Third Culture Kid" was first coined by sociologists John and Ruth Useem in the 1950s.[5] Back then, the term was limited to referencing children of American citizens who were working abroad. The Useems came up with this term after going to India and studying a group of Americans working there as foreign service officers and missionaries.

Ruth Useem defined the term *"third culture"* as "the styles of life created, shared, and learned by persons who are in the process of relating their societies, or sections thereof, to each other."[6]

Accordingly, a TCK would refer to children who have accompanied their parents in this process of assimilating and creating a "third culture" in another society.

This is a good point to clarify the term "third culture." Third in "third culture" does not refer to the number of countries or cultures that you have been exposed to. Put differently,

---

5    David C. Pollock, Ruth E. Van Reken, and Michael V. Pollock, *Third Culture Kids: Growing Up Among Worlds* (Boston: Nicholas Brealey Publishing, 2010), 39-46.

6    Ibid.

you cannot be a "fourth" or "fifth" culture kid because you have lived in more than three countries.

As Useem puts it, your first culture refers to home or the passport culture of your parents. Your second culture refers to the "host culture," or, in other words, the culture of the society in which you live. Your third culture, then, is not a preexisting culture. Instead, it is a "way of life" that is different from both your first and second cultures. It is a whole different culture that you have invented for yourself, yet, is shared by others who also go through a similar experience.

The specific term, "Third Culture Kid," was popularized in the famous book *Third Culture Kids: Growing Up Among Worlds,* published back in 1999 and written by sociologist David Pollock and coauthor Ruth E. Van Reken.

The definition provided in this first book remains the primary definition for the term Third Culture Kid. In the book, Pollock defines "Third Culture Kid" as follows:

*A person who has spent a significant part of [their] developmental years outside the parents' culture. The TCK frequently builds relationships to all of the cultures, while not having full ownership in any. Although elements from each culture may be assimilated into the TCK's life experience, the sense of belonging is [often] in relationship to others of similar background.*[7]

Let's take a moment to break down this definition.

---

7    Ibid., 15.

A TCK:

a. has grown up outside of their parents' culture (not counting infancy, since that would not be "significant developmental years")
b. built their societal relationships around all of the cultures they have been exposed to
c. has no ownership of any one culture
d. feels most comfortable around other TCKs, because they do not fully belong in any one culture

## CAN YOU RELATE?

If elements of the definition above ring true to your experience, you are probably a Third Culture Kid. Do take note that like all sociological terms, the definition is always fluid and changing. Not everyone who has experience growing up abroad will necessarily feel the same way about themselves (as you will soon find out from the awesome TCKs interviewed in this book), and nobody should ever label you or box you into a term that doesn't feel right to you.

Yet, the term and its definition still remain useful for those who do identify with it.

My favorite part of the definition is that a TCK's sense of belonging is often found in interacting with other TCKs. Even when I meet another TCK who has had an entirely different experience from mine—they could be born and raised in a whole different continent than I was—I can always empathize with them and have something to talk about. In other words, the term is useful in that it clarifies a community of people who can support each other, because we all understand what it feels like to "not belong" anywhere.

Coming to learn that my experience has a title and there's an entire community of people just like me all over the globe felt like a final piece of my personal identity puzzle. I went from being the outsider, the foreigner, the expat, and the nomad to having something to confidently claim as my own: the TCK identity.

## NAMING A SHARED EXPERIENCE

One of the first people who gave language to this very idea of the "TCK" was Ruth Van Reken. As I mentioned earlier, she is the coauthor of the first popular book on TCKs, *Third Culture Kids: Growing Up Among Worlds.*

Ruth was born and raised in Nigeria under American parents. Her father was also a TCK who was born and raised in Iran, known as Persia at the time. Ruth returned to the United States at the age of thirteen, only to discover that the culture she thought was her own really was not.

"I went back [to the States] assuming that I was from that culture, but I realized that I didn't know much about it. . . So after a year, when I went to high school, I decided that I wouldn't tell anybody I was from Nigeria or that I had ever been there."

Even when her parents moved back to Africa when she was a freshman in high school, Ruth remained in the States to finish school in the American curriculum. She finished high school in America, went to college in America, and married an American man.

In his senior year, Ruth's husband tried to go to Nigeria for his short-term elective, but Nigeria refused to give the couple a visa. Instead, they moved to Liberia. That difficult process, Ruth remembers, was her first "journey of verification"—a time when her memories of Nigeria were challenged.

When she returned to St. Louis and had her baby, Ruth went through depression for the first time in her life. Looking back, she realized this was because she never properly said goodbye to her life and memories in Africa.

"I'm sure now it was because I had touched the African side, but I never processed it. And grief goes into depression or anger. So, it's a protection against grief in many ways, which I didn't know [about at that time]. I just blamed everything around me. I blamed my husband's schedule and many other things in my life."

A few years later, the family moved back to Liberia. Although things started looking better after they moved back to Africa, Ruth experienced depression for the second time when her daughter moved away and the political situation made it difficult to stay in Africa, leading her to start writing. She started journaling her thoughts and revisiting the memories and feelings she never allowed herself to touch before.

Along that journey, she met Dave Pollock, the pioneering sociologist who had first developed the idea of the Third Culture Kid profile. Together, they published their first book,

*Third Culture Kids: The Experience of Growing Up Among Worlds* in 1999.

Since then, Ruth has traveled to over fifty countries to spread the idea of the TCK around the world. Her books, articles, lectures, and programs give language to a profound idea that was never understood or valued by monocultural communities.

The term "TCK" spurred the TCK community, which allowed the entire globe to be "home" for TCKs.

"It's just amazing because every place I go, I am affirmed again in my own story. I meet people who understand me the minute I'm back in an international environment."

Her favorite memory from her years of seminars around the world is from fifteen years ago when she went to lead a TCK panel at a school in the Hague.

With ten people on the panel to present, Ruth was pressed on time. Yet, the moment she saw an adorable little boy waving at her from the audience, she felt she needed to ask what he had to say.

The ten-year-old boy stood up, introduced himself, and said the following words:

"When I went back to Portugal, and my cousin said I wasn't Portuguese, I cried because, you know, I felt so bad."

Then he said, "I started to think about it. It's not true. I still am Portuguese, but I'm a TCK too."

Ruth recalls that those simple words from a small boy brought tears to the entire crowd. These are the moments that make Ruth do what she does.

That story that Ruth shared with me stayed with me for a long time too. It really is amazing how a single term can bring people together and give a name to something that so many people experience, including the ten-year-old boy who thought he was lacking something critical to his identity. For the first time, he had realized that he was not semi- or pseudo-Portuguese, but both Portuguese *and* a TCK. The term normalizes his experience and amplifies his identities. He is not lacking anything; instead, he has more identities than other Portuguese kids who have been raised in Portugal their whole lives.

This is the beautiful power of sharing our stories—with each other and with the world.

As Ruth put it, "I think the most amazing thing to me is that what seemed like my negative stuff has turned into my blessing. I think that's for all of us. We run from our pain, we run from our grief, and we run from the things that are hard. If we process that, I think we can use it as a blessing. . . I think somehow trying to understand my own story puts language on what happened."

## VARIATIONS OF THE "TCK"

At the conclusion of our interview together, Ruth compared the idea of the "TCK" to a Christmas tree. The branches have been built but the ornaments can be hung and taken off again and again.

The term "TCK" is constantly changing and evolving, as is the idea of the TCK. In fact, variations of the term TCK have developed over the years.

## THE ATCK

Ruth Van Reken and David Pollock adapted the original term "TCK" to apply to adults who grew up as TCKs; this term that they introduced is "adult TCKs," or *ATCK*s. According to Van Reken, ATCKs go through similar, yet somewhat different, difficulties from their younger counterparts.

ATCKs still struggle with the challenges of being a TCK from their childhood. Yet, because they are mature adults making a living for themselves, a lot of the internal challenges that built up from childhood, ranging from "depression, isolation, loneliness, anger, rebellion, and despair" often lead to a shell around them that even their closest friends and families cannot penetrate.[8] Many claim that they are fine, yet their experiences of being a TCK—often involving separation from family members, witnessing war, or conflicts in their host countries—remain points of "unresolved grief" that they constantly have to deal with.[9]

The central question and challenge for an ATCK, then, is whether they can "put these pieces together."[10]

---

8    Ibid., 15.

9    Ibid., 302.

10   Ibid.

Ruth goes on to answer that ATCKs most certainly can get over their unresolved grief and issues. In fact, she wrote a whole chapter on tips for struggling ATCKs. If you identify as an ATCK, I recommend that you check out the latest edition of Van Reken and Pollock's *Third Culture Kids*. Many interview excerpts and professional tips on resolving your inner grief as an adult TCK are included.

### THE CCK

Another relatively recent variation of the term TCK is the CCK, which stands for "Cross-Cultural Kid." Ruth came up with the term in 2002 to create a more inclusive term that can also apply to those who are not strictly a "TCK."

According to Ruth, a CCK is "a person who is living/has lived in—or meaningfully interacted with—two or more cultural environments for a significant period of time during their first eighteen years of life."[11]

Again, she has also coined a variation of the term to apply to adults: *ACCK*, short for "adult CCK."

The CCK not only includes the traditional TCK but also biracial children, children of immigrants, children of refugees, and international adoptees.[12] In other words, the CCK is a larger, more general term that includes other forms of multicultural experiences beyond just the TCK experience.

---

11   Ibid., 43.

12   Ibid.

If this is all very overwhelming for you, don't panic! The whole point of all these different terms, again, is to put a name to the experiences of marginalized people who grew up in different circumstances from the monocultural majority of the population.

Whether you identify as a TCK, an ATCK, a CCK, or an ACCK, we have all experienced common themes of "restlessness, little sense of personal identity, [and] unresolved grief due to recurrent losses"—something your monocultural friends or even family members might not quite understand.[13]

The most important takeaway here is that a TCK/CCK community exists. You are not alone in your fight with insecurities and uncertainties.

Even more importantly, your story *matters*. So, if you do not relate with the above terms, you are free to add your own ideas into the established conversation and decorate the TCK "Christmas tree," just as I will be doing in the following chapter.

---

13   Daniel Long, "Asian Third Culture Kids: A Phenomenological Study of the Cross-Cultural Identity of Chinese Students Educated in a Western-Curriculum International School," (PhD diss., Northeastern University, 2016), 19.

## THREE POINT SUMMARY

- A TCK is someone who has "spent a significant part of his or her developmental years outside the parents' culture."
- Having a term like this matters because it provides a language to our unique yet shared experiences and stories.
- The concept of the "TCK" is constantly expanding! Variations of the term include the ATCK (adult TCK), the CCK (cross-cultural kid), and the ACCK (adult CCK).

# CHAPTER 2:

# THE TCT

——

*"Everything was normal for me until I came back to the States for high school when I was thirteen. That's when the bottom fell out of my world for a bit. . . Thirteen is an ugly age. Nobody should be thirteen."*

— RUTH VAN REKEN

You have now learned about the many variations of the term "TCK," ranging from "ATCK" all the way to "CCK."

'Wait,' you might be thinking. 'But your book is titled *The Third Culture Teen*.'

Don't worry, I'm not scamming you with some made-up word.

Actually, I kind of am because the term I will propose to you now is a brand-new term that has not been shared with the world before.

This is my contribution to the "Christmas Tree": the Third Culture Teen, or the TCT for short.

Being a teenager, in general, is a time of great conflict and confusion in one's identity. This is especially true for a TCK who has grown up with clashing cultures their entire life.

I believe these few years of being both a TCK and a teenager—a TCT—is significant enough to be differentiated from the established terms of a TCK or an ATCK. Here's why.

### HOW A TCT IS DIFFERENT FROM A TCK

While living outside my passport country was definitely a challenge, I viewed it more as an adventure throughout my childhood. I have a rose-colored view of my childhood as a TCK because I was sheltered by my parents for the majority of my TCK life.

Author Rachel Pieh Jones, the mother of TCK children who were raised in Djibouti in East Africa, shared a similar story with me during our interview.

"I remember one time I said, kind of under my breath, that I'm so tired of living in Djibouti. My youngest daughter was completely taken back by this, asking, 'what?' Living here was extra stress, but [that stress] never occurred to her, so there's definitely a different experience [between hers and mine]."

Only when Rachel's children grew older and had to deal with this "extra stress" themselves—ranging from exchanging money, applying for passports, and paying taxes in multiple countries—did they truly understand the difficulties of living abroad. Rachel emphasizes that this is the core difference between being a "kid" and being a "teenager."

"As a kid, you're sheltered from [these stressors] and you should be. That leaves a kind of space for the kids to experience only fun things like school and touring without any of those stressors."

Listening to Rachel's stories of her children reminded me of my struggles of growing up and having to face new "stressors" of my expat life.

When I look back at the time I spent in Malaysia and China, I can only recall fun experiences like taking swimming lessons in Malaysia or getting to try dumplings for the first time in China.

More importantly, I never felt very different from everybody else, because my earliest memories take place within an accepting international community. Surrounded by my fellow "foreigner" friends at school or fellow Korean families from my dad's workplace rather than the actual local population, I rarely felt out of place in my daily life.

My parents did everything: the speaking, the taxes, and the visas—all the way to searching for the right school where I could feel comfortable. It never occurred to me that I was different from everybody else and that it may be difficult to live in a foreign land surrounded by foreigners. The feeling of unbelonging and the difficulty of living abroad only really hit me when I grew older and left my safe space consisting of my family and my international school friends.

Many other TCTs I have interviewed went through similar significant transitions in their lives as they grew older. These transitions often include going to a new high school, finding a job, or, as in my case, moving into college. For the first time, these teens have to face the fact that they are different from everybody else. And this time, their family is not there to help them through it. Teenage years, especially late teen years, are, hence, an especially particular and difficult time for these TCKs.

Here are some of these stories of transition.

When asked what point in their lives their children struggled with the most due to their cultural background, Rachel answered,

"When they were sophomores in university, connecting to their American culture [was very difficult for them]. They look like they're from Minnesota but inside they don't feel like Americans, so they had a hard time knowing how to connect with people and how to make friends. That transition period has probably been the hardest."

Jessica Kim, a TCT born in Korea, raised in Taiwan, and currently in Los Angeles for college, also shared a similar story about the concerns she had before leaving her home in Taiwan for the first time.

"I think, like many international school kids, I was very used to my close group of friends. I went to the same school from first grade to twelfth grade, and we just had sixty people per grade. I've seen [my classmates] since they were babies. I've seen them go through puberty and I've seen their parents. We were able to talk about things most friends have a hard time talking about, like family issues or mental health issues. I was very thankful for that, but I also knew that I was in a very unique environment. So, I was very worried about college. I was very comfortable in high school. It was hard for me to go to college and leave my town and my school."

Ruth, as discussed in the earlier chapter, also went through a significant transition as a TCT: moving to the United States.

"I enjoyed my life enormously in Nigeria. Everything was normal for me until I came back to the States for high school when I was thirteen. That's when the bottom fell out of my world for a bit. Living in the States, I had realized that although I had always assumed I was part of the American culture, I did not know much about it."

"It was even worse because I was thirteen. Thirteen is an ugly age. Nobody should be thirteen."

As seen from the stories above, the TCT experience is different from the TCK experience because your transition from childhood to adulthood—often paired with a literal physical transition—provides a new perspective on one's life as a TCK.

Only when you step out of the comforts of your parents and the comforts of your international community does the real difficulty of being a "Third Culture" person really hit you.

For instance, you have to learn to make friends from mono-cultural backgrounds. Many TCTs resort to putting on a mask belonging to a certain culture so they can fit in with the crowd. This comes with abbreviating their background—even though the abbreviated version of where they are from may not feel comfortable to them.

All the while, they need to go through the same challenges of growing into an adult—getting a driver's license, learning how to cook food, or getting their first job. . .

For a lot of TCTs, including myself, these are all in addition to adapting to a new environment such as college.

Just as a ten-year-old child's experience under the roof of their parents is very different from an eighteen-year-old teen's experience at a university, the TCT experience should be differentiated from the TCK experience.

## HOW A TCT IS DIFFERENT FROM AN ATCK
Just as the TCT experience is different from the TCK experience, the TCT experience is also very different from the ATCK's experience.

A TCT is different from an ATCK in that the lives of TCTs are relatively more fluid and uncertain.

This is not to claim that ATCKs do not experience transitions or that they are too old to resolve their internal struggles. However, ATCKs have, despite their unresolved identity crises, most often settled into a stationary adult lifestyle. Most factors of their lives, including where they live, what they want to do, or the close group of people in their lives, have been established. In this sense, they live a somewhat similar life as a TCK in that they have established a circle of family and friends who are willing to listen to their stories.

Returning to Ruth's first instance of depression, Ruth's struggles as an ATCK got circumstantially better after she settled into a stable life with her husband in Liberia.

"When I went back to the States and I had a new baby, I had depression for the first time in my life. . . But [our family] moved to Liberia and things were better circumstantially. We went back to Liberia for my husband to work as a doctor there, and I was fine."

She discussed how having her husband by her side and starting a family of her own helped her feel more settled and secure. Her second instance of depression did not hit her until her daughter left the family for college, leading to a significant change within her family.

As teenagers become adults, they develop a more mature view of others, which also makes the expat experience much easier for ATCKs than for TCTs.

Lindie Botes, an ATCK born in South Africa, raised in France, Pakistan and the UAE, and currently based in Singapore, recalls how her decision to quit her job and leave South Africa as an adult was different from her teenage days of going to school in Dubai.

"I think when I had my first job in South Africa, that's when I knew I did not want to settle in South Africa. I knew it was just a temporary time to get some job experience. I decided not to invest in building [unnecessary relationships] since I knew I was going to leave."

Lindie noted that such decision to limit her social circle would not have been possible back when she was a teen.

"In high school, you're so young and you need many friends to thrive whereas when you're an adult it's okay if you [just] have one or two close friends."

As seen in Lindie's story, a teenager's priorities often differ from those of an adult. Most teenagers prioritize fitting in to a mass of friends rather than taking the time to explore who they are and carefully selecting the people they truly want in their lives. TCTs, hence, face bigger struggles in adjusting to the environment around them.

Many ATCKs, having moved past the turbulent stage of being a TCT, also have a stronger sense of cultural identity. They can easily accept their TCK identity, which is an issue many TCTs constantly struggle with.

Kawtar El Alaoui, an ATCK currently working as a cross-cultural trainer, for instance, embraced and took advantage of her experience of growing up as a TCK to advance her career after she became an adult.

"My lifestyle for the last seven years has been really just a global nomad. I've lived in South Korea for four years. Now I'm living in Mumbai, India, and it's been almost three years. Culture has become such an important part of my identity that it's also part of what I do for work."

The stability, acceptance, and confidence that comes with growing into an adult and settling into a set lifestyle differentiate an ATCK from a TCT.

## THE TCT PROFILE

Now that we know how a TCT is different from a TCK and an ATCK, I will delineate some of the unique experiences and challenges that TCTs face. These topics will be individually delved into in depth as the book progresses.

### 1. FITTING IN

As Lindie mentioned, fitting in is especially a great concern for TCTs. Teenagers have been scientifically proven to care more about how they are viewed by their peers than children or adults.

According to Isabelle Rosso of the Harvard Medical School, teenagers' prefrontal cortexes massively rebuild and develop in preparation for adulthood, leading to their dramatically increased ability to "look at themselves the way they feel other people are looking at them."[14] This heightened sense of self "[allows teens] to have more social self-consciousness, and worry more about what other people are thinking about [them]. It may open up new vulnerabilities in some adolescents."[15]

New vulnerabilities are dangerous discoveries for Third Culture Teens who already deal with the trouble of finding a sense of belonging. Third Culture Teens' brains are physically wired to want to belong in an established community, making the expat experience uniquely more difficult for them.

### 2. ADULTING

Adulting does not only involve learning to do laundry on your own for the first time for TCTs.

Adulting also means learning to deal with the monocultural world beyond the comforts of your international community of friends and family for the first time.

Many TCTs move to a non-international community and are faced with challenges they have never faced before.

Their heads are filled with questions about how they should behave in front of monocultural friends.

---

14   Erika Packard, "That teenage feeling: Harvard researchers may have found biological clues to quirky adolescent behavior," *American Psychological Association* 38, no. 4 (2007).

15   Ibid.

How do you introduce yourself when nobody else has a complicated background like you do? How do you deal with people who have drastically different worldviews from you?

Learning these new social skills, in addition to growing into an adult on your own, is a crucial part of the TCT experience.

### 3. LEAVING HOME AND SEARCHING FOR A NEW HOME

While home may have always been a fluid concept for TCKs, for TCTs, the meaning of home gets even *more* complicated because many of them leave their families for the first time.

Entities isolated from the rest of their families, they now have their own homes in addition to the homes that their families are living in—all in addition to the numerous places around the globe that they have previously identified as home.

They face the challenge of reflecting back on all the homes they have had in their lives while they try to discover a new home for themselves.

### 4. TECHNOLOGY

Technology has drastically changed the experience of being a TCK in recent years.

Many TCTs of the previous generation have not faced both the advantages and challenges of having accessible technology as a teen. Technology plays an especially important role for TCTs in this generation because it connects people and places that once felt distant and permanently separated.

Balancing the benefits and challenges that come with technology is a crucial part of the modern TCT experience.

* * *

Above is the portrayal of the TCT profile—a struggling, globally nomadic teen trying to find their place in this world for the first time.

I will be discussing the specific experiences that TCTs have, the specific challenges that they face, and more importantly, how to cope with them to grow to be a happier, more confident ATCK.

First of all, as a quick disclaimer, despite the discrepancies delineated, TCTs have more commonalities with TCKs and ATCKs than differences. Because of this, I will be interchanging terms such as TCTs and TCKs in certain parts of the book where I find applicable.

More importantly, while TCT is a term that I have invented to describe a specific experience, it is not a rigid term. Life works differently in various stages for everyone, and childhood, adolescence, and adulthood work not in perfectly separated stages but in gradients. A TCK might feel like a TCT even though they technically are not a "teen" yet or an ATCK may discover that they still go through the struggles of a TCT although they have grown past adolescence. This is perfectly normal, and you should not feel in any way discouraged because you are not part of the perfect TCT profile.

The whole point of the term "TCT" is that people can feel recognized and identified for who they are. Terms as such should always be more inclusive rather than cast people out.

A Third Culture Teen is a new term that we need to accept for the sake of millions of struggling Third Culture Teens around the globe. Recognizing their identity as TCTs can help them greatly in understanding the specific challenges they face as a Third Culture Teen and help them advance further in life with the advantages they have as TCTs.

This way, when TCTs grow into ATCKs, they can be more comfortable with living in their own skin as they venture out into the world on their own.

## THREE POINT SUMMARY

- A "TCT" is a Third Culture Teen.
- TCTs are different from TCKs in that they make significant transitions in life without their family, shedding out of the rose-colored expat experiences that TCKs have.
- TCTs are different from ATCKs in that they do not have a stable home, family, or life plan yet. TCTs are venturing out into the world on their own for the first time.

# PART 2:

# THE ISSUES
# WE FACE

# CHAPTER 3:

# HOME

——

*"I build my home in the hearts of people."*

—ISABELLE MIN

Below is the definition of the word "home" in the New Oxford American Dictionary.

**HOME | HŌM | NOUN**

The place where one lives *permanently* [emphasis added], especially as a member of a *family* [emphasis added] or household.[16]

Here lies the fundamental paradox of "home" for a Third Culture Teen: no such place where one lives "permanently" exists. Yet, "home"—somewhere to rely on and miss—is such a fundamental concept for all human beings; it may perhaps even be a primal desire that we have all been born with.

---

16    *New Oxford English Dictionary,* 2nd ed, s.v. "Home."

Because of this, TCTs are in a constant search for what this mysterious word "home" might mean in their lives.

Third Culture Teens all develop their own ways to cope with such a paradox. I have gathered excerpts of my conversations with TCTs and ATCKs and organized them into different categories the word "home" might mean to them. I hope that these categorizations help clarify the concept "home" a bit more for you.

## 1. NOT A PHYSICAL LOCATION BUT THE PEOPLE

From the interviews I have conducted, I have noticed that many TCTs and ATCKs turn to people rather than physical locations to define as home.

A common point of reference is family.

For instance, here is an answer from Kayla Cao, a Canadian TCT raised in China, about where home is for her.

"Home is wherever my mom is. Because I move around a lot, I don't get attached to geographical places. You have to know that those places do not exist without your family. These places, and the memories you have of them, are dependent on your family.

"So, home is where my family is [right now]. When people ask me [where home is], I answer that my mom's in Beijing and my siblings are in New York."

For Kayla, home is a fluid concept. It is not one permanently designated physical location, but wherever her family members are living at the moment. In other words, "home" for her directly corresponds to her family.

Lindie Botes gave a similar answer regarding the question of home.

"No place ever really feels right, and I don't think we'll ever find that place. *But the people really make it. . .* It's my home, the cooking, my church, and my family . . . so what I would call home is wherever I feel most comfortable.

"Home is very fluid, and I don't consider there being one home. I have many homes mentally and emotionally in different parts of the world."

Isabelle Min, a Korean ATCK born in the United States and raised in Brazil, Italy, and Libya, put it succinctly as such:

"I build my home in the hearts of people."

## 2. NOT A PHYSICAL LOCATION BUT A FEELING OF BELONGING

For some TCKs, certain people are not who make a home a home, but the feeling of comfort and belonging that instantly makes a place a "home."

Here's a take from Amy McMillen, a US-born ATCK raised in China, on home.

"I think when I'm in an environment where there're different types of people, I feel more comfortable and more at home— more belonging."

She used the example of her group of friends in college. While they were all from different backgrounds and different countries, being surrounded by them instantly made her feel "at home." On the other hand, when she is surrounded by a more homogenous group of people from the same background, she always feels othered and out of place.

She also recalled her solo trip to Italy. While she had never been to Italy and the people she met there were all strangers, she felt at home because she was in a comfortable group of people from different backgrounds.

"It's not the location that gives me those feelings of home . . ."

"It's little moments where I feel like I'm exactly where I'm supposed to be, and that feels more like home to me than anything else."

What is especially interesting to point out here is that Amy also feels at home, ironically, in an entirely foreign environment such as Italy—simply because she is exposed to a diversity of people and cultures. This stands in contrast with mostly white, suburban Virginia, where she had lived for the longest portion of her life, and hence, the "home" most people expect her to identify with.

Ruth brought up a similar point when she reflected back on her experience of traveling across the globe and interacting with different TCK communities.

"I have one life here and then I get on a plane, I go there, and another minute, I'm in that community—wherever it is, whatever country it's in, I feel at home. I think it's interesting that the feeling of home is different from where you're from. Feeling at home is a *place of feeling*. I think home is the feeling of being accepted and comfortable and understood."

Although Ruth already has a physical home in the United States where she has lived with her family for decades—the literal "home" where she has permanently settled in for a long time—Ruth says that she feels at home when she gets out of that home and immerses herself into other TCK communities around the world.

This is, again, where we can see the importance of a TCK community. The reason why everyone looks for the feeling of home is so that they *belong* somewhere. They have somewhere to comfortably call their own.

Going back to the first category of home, that is why many TCKs identify a group of people as their "home." This group of people makes them feel welcomed. For Kayla and many other TCKs, this would be their family. Wherever your family members are, seeing them and spending time with them make you feel as if you belong there. For others, it might be a group of friends or other community of reliable people. Sometimes, as in the case of Amy, this community of people could be total strangers who might share a similar experience to you.

Those of you who do not have friends and family to turn to, I recommend that you seek the TCK community to call home—whether it be in person or online. We all share the common feeling of not belonging, and we can be found in every continent of the planet. Sometimes, having the feeling of unbelonging validated by others might feel more like "home" than being at an actual, physical location labeled home. Having the TCK community allows anyone, even if they don't have close friends or family near them, to find help through difficult times and to have a home for themselves.

Refer to Chapter 9 for how to find and/or create your own TCK community.

## 3-1. A PHYSICAL LOCATION (EVEN WHEN IT'S NOT YOUR PASSPORT COUNTRY)

For other TCKs, even after moving to different countries all their lives, they might still identify a single physical location as their home.

If you're lucky, that place might be your "literal" home—also known as your passport country.

For instance, Kawtar, who has a Canadian passport, still identifies Canada as her home regardless of the countries she has lived in throughout her life.

"I actually didn't find a home externally until I found it internally. For me, that big shift happened when I started coaching as a career. I started looking into who I am on a deeper level and my real values versus the ones I adopted from my cultures. . ."

"Through coaching, I explored my cultural identities and identified where it intersected with my core values versus where I had adopted cultural narratives as mine to try to fit it. I discovered through that exploration that Canada is home for me. My family's there, and it is where my heart is. This exploration also created space for me to make peace with my relationship with my culture of origin and cultivate a conscious sense of belonging to each of them from my core."

This was the same for Fareeha Mahmood, a Bangladesh-born TCK.

"My freshman year [of college], a lot of people would ask me, 'Where is home?' It was always a confusing question to answer. At the time, my parents were still living in Dubai, UAE, and that city was my home for the longest time—that is where I grew up, met some of my closest friends, and became confident in who I am. Dubai will always hold a special place in my heart. But, at the same time, I always felt close to my Bengali identity and culture. There were certainly some ups and downs, but I still consider Dhaka, Bangladesh my home. Even when I lived in Dubai, when I travelled to Dhaka for winter or summer break, I would tell people I'm going home."

"I don't necessarily think home has to be equated to where you live the longest. I think it's the place that you have the strongest connection to whether it be familial or cultural.

"Later, at the end of freshman year when my parents moved back to Dhaka, Bangladesh, I think that made it easier to tell people I was from Dhaka and it was my home instead of having to explain all the places I've lived. I always look forward to going back to Dhaka to spend time with my parents, my brother, my cousins, my uncles, and aunts. Dhaka for me is definitely home."

For Kawtar and Fareeha, their passport countries are still their homes. But not necessarily because they were simply born there. As they have both shared in their stories, they identify with their passport country because their personal values align with the values found there.

For Kawtar, she identified more with the relatively liberal, Western ideals found in Canada. In her teenage years, she felt restricted by the Moroccan values that her father expected of her. Seeing how she divided the journey of finding home through two processes is interesting—the internal and the external. The physical manifestation of the "external" home only came to her after she had settled on an internal home— the culture she identifies with, the goals she wants to pursue in life, the country she feels most connected with, and more.

Similarly for Fareeha, even after living in Dubai, earlier years of her life in Indonesia, and in New York City for college, she feels that fundamental parts of her identity are still very Bengali. Hence, regardless of where she has previously lived and where she will be living in the future, she will always identify Dhaka, Bangladesh, as her home.

The situation gets a little more complicated when the physical location you identify with is not your passport country.

Here is Jessica Kim's story. Although she was born in Korea, she has spent most of her lifetime in Taiwan.

"I went to my sister to see how I should feel about where home is because she was in the same predicament as me right now, and she went through it earlier in her life. She never considered Taiwan her home, so I thought if I leave Taiwan [as she did] I'm never going to consider this place my home."

However, upon leaving Taiwan for the first time to start college in the United States, Jessica felt an even stronger attachment to Taiwan.

"My freshman year I missed home and when I missed home, it was Taiwan. Taiwan is the only place where I have real memories of growing up in contrast to Korea where I only have memories of visiting during vacation."

Upon realizing that the true home for her is Taiwan, she also discovered why she could never confidently claim that Taiwan is home for her while she was growing up there.

"I also realized I have been holding on to an idealized version of Korea. Whenever something was wrong in Taiwan, I just was like, oh, if I had grown up in Korea, maybe it would have been better."

However, simply realizing that Taiwan is her home is not the end of the problem for her.

"I think now I feel more comfortable saying that Taiwan is my home. Now, that is another problem because Taiwan is such a homogenous community. You can't just say you are Taiwanese because you live in Taiwan."

In Jessica's case, she identifies Taiwan as her home, but she knows that she can never be called Taiwanese just because she lives in the country. She does not have citizenship there, let alone permanent residency. Moreover, unlike other countries in the West, many Asian countries, including Taiwan, are racially and culturally homogenous. Many Asian countries still have difficulty with accepting that a different-looking person speaking a different language could be a part of their national community.

This also leads to confusion from non-TCKs who do not quite understand that your "home" could be different from where you were born. Jessica regretfully recalls how whenever she tells strangers that she is "from Taiwan," they automatically assume that she is Taiwanese.

Jessica's story demonstrates the importance of TCK representation in the world. The state of being "from" somewhere yet not being a citizen of that country should be more normalized. When one answers that they are "from" a certain place, assumptions about their nationality or race should not follow.

We have the freedom to choose where to be "from."

## 3-2. A PHYSICAL LOCATION (BUT YOU ARE GOING THROUGH TRANSITIONS)

Sometimes, the concept of home is even more complicated for TCTs, not only because of their transition, but their family's. As seen earlier, family plays a big role in determining where you believe your home is. For TCTs, many of whom now live separately from their parents, they may have to go through unwanted psychological transitions because of their family's physical transitions.

Take the instance of my family.

Although my dad worked in Qingdao, China, when I was graduating high school in Qingdao, he moved to Qinhuangdao in northern China for work.

However, the rest of my family (my mom and my sister) decided to remain in Qingdao. This is because my sister had only two years left of high school by the time my dad transferred, and my mom thought my sister would be better off remaining in the same school for both academic and emotional reasons.

Now that my sister will be graduating this summer, the question of where my family will be is completely up in the air. My dad might continue to work in northern China. He is also thinking about looking for a new job in a new city or perhaps even a new country, but none of these things have been decided yet.

This means that my "home"—where my family is—would change twice during my college years.

I "returned home" to an unfamiliar apartment for my summer break freshman year because my mom and my sister moved to a smaller apartment after my dad and I moved out.

Summer of my sophomore year, my sister would be off to college and my parents would be living somewhere entirely new.

A lot of my friends from high school went through something similar. To help their kids graduate in the same school they had been attending, even when the dads moved away to a new country or back to their home country, many of the moms still chose to remain in Qingdao. That meant as soon as the kid graduated high school, the rest of the family would move to wherever the dad went.

A child's transition through school, a lot of which happens in their teenage years, greatly affects the family as a whole. This makes "home" an even more difficult concept for Third Culture Teens: not just because they have had homes in different countries, but also because their homes are *literally* changing as their families and they themselves move away.

"Home" has always just felt like Qingdao to me. I think this is largely because I have, returning to David Pollock's definition of the Third Culture Kid, spent all of my "*developmental years*" in Qingdao.

I was born in Korea and was raised in Korea until I moved to Kuala Lumpur, Malaysia, when I was nine years old. I was there until fourth grade. Yet, all of those memories feel like a blur to me. I only remember bits and pieces of what my kindergarten years in Korea were like, and my memory of school life in Malaysia is clearer yet still minimal.

I then moved to Qingdao, China, and went to school there until sixth grade. I remember that a lot more clearly. I think that was because those were my "developmental" preteen years.

During this time, I (wrongly) chose career paths for my future, going through phases of wanting to be the next Hannah Montana, the next Meg Cabot, and even a cartoonist. This was also the time when I had a crush on somebody for the first time and when I met my favorite teacher, who encouraged me to write for the rest of my life.

After spending a few years in Seoul, Korea, and a year of boarding school in Cheonan, Korea, I moved back to the same school in Qingdao to finish high school. That was another "developmental" couple of teenage years when I (although I'm still *clearly* in the process of doing so) matured into an adult. I spent those years thinking of larger "adult" questions I carried on through college, including my (actual) career path, my worldview, and my religion.

Even when the apartment that my mom and my sister lived in changed and I couldn't remember the proper address to my new "home" in Qingdao all throughout summer break, I was still glad to return to Qingdao. Whenever anyone in college asked where I was from, I would answer "China," even if that meant people wrongly assumed I was Chinese.

I love coming back and knowing where my favorite restaurants are.

I love coming back and knowing where my favorite spot to walk my dog is.

I think I just love the idea of "coming back" somewhere because so much of my life is constantly changing, and I really need that one "constant" in life.

I talked this through with my mom—how I always felt like Qingdao was the one home in my life. Upon hearing this, my mom, the most supportive mom in the world, opened up a serious family conversation and suggested that my dad get a new job in Qingdao or even take out loans just to keep an apartment in Qingdao for me to come back to.

Yet, growing up and becoming more aware of the troubles of my parents, I realized that Qingdao is not home for my parents. This was especially the case for my mom who struggled through the last couple of years trying to raise my sister on her own. I remember trying to hold down a sob when she told me that she has too many bad memories of struggle in Qingdao and would like to leave the city as soon as possible. Moreover, I knew finding new jobs or new houses in China was extremely difficult for foreigners.

I came to a realization that I was extremely selfish in trying to convince my parents to stay in Qingdao just for me to have a home. How was I to ask them to have a home in a city where they did not feel comfortable just so I could come back to a place of comfort for three weeks over break?

It's still a hard pill for me to swallow, and thinking of leaving this place—for real, permanently, this time—makes me sadder than anything else in the world.

For Third Culture Teens in expat families like my own, I have to say having the more abstract, fluid definition of a "home" is healthy. That way, even when your home changes while you are away and you can no longer return to a place of comfort, you can still feel comfortable in a whole different place. I try to think in that direction too and that is what my mom advises as well.

But, no matter how many times you've done it, leaving home is really hard.

## 4. WHEN YOU DON'T WANT A HOME

Other times, especially for TCTs going through transitions, not having a home is just healthier.

As many TCKs have attested, one of our biggest struggles is not when we move to a different country but when we return to the country we are supposed to belong in.

This was true for me when I had to move back to Seoul, Korea, for middle school. I had an especially difficult time because I was bullied back in my school in China by a group of Korean girls. Looking back, I think that developed into a form of utter *fear* of Korea. I remember bawling and begging my mom for us to stay in Qingdao.

But of course, just like how life abroad was thrown at me without a choice, it was taken away from me just as easily. I had no choice in deciding whether our family could stay in China.

For the first time, I had to wear a uniform to school. To make matters worse, my middle school in Korea was a strict private school with rules on how short your hair could be, how short your nails could be, and even the color of socks you were allowed to wear in certain months of the year.

Having spent the past five years in an American school system, this was not something I was used to at all. I was the first kid in the entire grade who got detention for not cutting my hair short enough in time for hair length examination.

I was constantly whining about life in Korea. Every morning I would wake up and my first question at the breakfast table would be "when are we going abroad again?" I couldn't wait to get out of there and escape the group of people who looked like me yet hated me for being so different.

One day after school, my mom had made some changes to the kitchen. First, I noticed a new sign posted on the fridge:

"WE ARE ON A LONG VACATION."

Next to the sign was a big map of the world with little red dots in random spots of the globe.

"What *is* this?" I asked my mom, taking off my brand-new mandatory leather dress shoes.

"It is what it says," she answered.

"We don't live here. We are not going to settle here. This is just a long vacation. We are tourists here in Seoul. And these . . ."

She pointed to the map.

"Are all the places Dad can potentially be transferred to from his company. It could be LA." She pointed at the American continent.

"Or it could be Dubai." Her finger moved to the UAE.

"Or it could be back to Malaysia. Who knows?" Her finger landed on Southeast Asia.

I first thought it was all just a bogus scheme of hers to make me feel better. But our entire family, from that day on and for the following three and a half years, lived like tourists in the city.

From the landmark of Seoul, the N Seoul Tower, to the traditional palaces like Gyeong-bok-goong, all the way to the beaches in southern Korean cities like Busan, I have literally been everywhere in Seoul and beyond. I have been to more places in Korea than most of my friends who were born and raised in Korea ever have.

Every weekend was an adventure regardless of whether I had assignments or exams. Our fridge started filling up with cheesy tourist souvenirs—from big "SEOUL" magnets to a picture of the Korean flag.

Thinking back, ironically enough, I don't think I would be feeling this strong connection to Korea if my mom didn't encourage us to act like tourists. She didn't force my sister and me to adapt to the Korean lifestyle. Instead, she embraced the foreignness of our experiences and let us enjoy the best parts of Korea as ourselves.

The side effect of that must be what Dr. Schuilenberg describes in *Finding Home*: "[Idealization] of a particular time/place."[17]

All that's left of me in my adult brain are the fun memories my family had together in Korea, many of which Koreans who were raised in Korea all their lives can't relate to. Images of Korea for me remain as exciting superficial flashes a tourist would see rather than the actual realities and social conditions that define the communal Korean experience.

Perhaps my mom didn't present me with the most authentic Korean experience, but now that I'm living abroad again (as I had so dearly wished back in middle school), having somewhere to miss is really nice.

\* \* \*

So where do *you* identify as home (if you even want to have the idea of a "home" in the first place)?

---

17   Susannah-Joy Schuilenberg, "A Whole Self," in *Finding Home: Third Culture Kids in the World,* ed. Rachel Pieh Jones (Washington: Amazon, 2018), 922-1048.

Regardless of what category of answers yours belong to—a place, people, a feeling, or perhaps, even nothing—what matters is that you have somewhere to rely on at difficult times.

As TCTs, we are burdened with the fate of being rootless. We have to go through many more transitions and, accordingly, struggles that many monocultural teenagers do not have to face.

You should never have to go through this alone. Always consult with and keep in touch with your family if you define them as your home. If not, find and make a community of people who could be your home—your friends, a student organization, a church, or any group of people you can rely on. If that is not possible in the circumstances you are in right now, make the opportunity to venture out and discover comfort for yourself. It could be going on a solo trip as Amy did, or it could even be taking a short walk to a serene park nearby where you feel most at peace.

We never have to have the "home" Oxford dictionary defines—who cares what they say? But we, like everybody else, *do* need a home, even if that will look very different from the "home" other kids may identify with.

Where/what/who is your home?

## THREE POINT SUMMARY

- Home can be people, a feeling, or even a place.
- Sometimes, you might even decide not to have a home.
- But our lives are constantly changing—have a home of some sort to rely on.

# CHAPTER 4:

# AN INTERVIEW WITH GRACE LEE

————

*"Really try to make good, quality memories and be kind to other people. Because your home may change and your high school campus may change, and the teachers might change, but that spirit will still be there. That's what remains."*

—GRACE LEE

Life as a TCK is a series of goodbyes.

This is especially the case for Third Culture Teens who are experiencing even more emotional and physical transitions in their lives. During such times, remembering that the people and places you leave behind are not gone forever is helpful.

Grace Lee, a high school English teacher at the International School of Qingdao (ISQ) and an ATCK, shared with me the importance of making and reflecting back upon memories as a TCK.

Grace—or Ms. Lee—is my sister's Advanced Placement Literature teacher. She came to Qingdao to teach in 2018, so I did not get to know her while I went to school in Qingdao. When my sister told me about Ms. Lee also being a TCK, I asked for an interview—to which she agreed to right away.

Returning to my high school for the interview was an interesting experience. I think the first emotion that struck me was a remorseful kind of sadness. I had to get a guest pass at the gate instead of showing my student ID to the guard at the gate. Although the building was the same on the outside, the staircase had new paintings on them, and the auditorium walls included unfamiliar additions to the row of high school drama production posters.

Upon meeting Grace and moving to her classroom to talk, I passed by many teachers I had never seen before. In the classroom, the tables and chairs looked smaller than I remembered them, and the assignments written on the board looked almost foreign, even though I sat in the same chairs and took the same class just a couple of years ago.

It struck me that so many things in the school had changed and the ISQ that I graduated from no longer existed.

When we sat on the couch in Grace's classroom to talk, however, I felt a sense of familiarity grow back in my heart. It might not have been the familiarity of high school or my memories from it, but our bond together as a TCK immediately made me feel at ease.

Grace was born in Korea but moved to Chiang Mai, Thailand when she was three months old. She lived there with her family until she graduated high school, upon which she moved to Michigan in the United States for college. She went through two additional transitions after college, moving first to Indonesia, then to Yantai, China, and finally Qingdao, China, where she is teaching today.

Just as many Third Culture Teens, including myself, have, Grace experienced her first identity crisis when she moved to the United States for the first time for college. She attended a small private Christian college in Michigan and was the only Korean student there.

"A lot of my classmates were from a forty-five-minute drive away from college. I didn't know how to explain myself. I think when I went to a context where people didn't understand what it meant to move, I really struggled with it."

For Grace, the struggle did not, however, just have to do with being from some place far from campus. It was also from being from multiple places at the same time.

"I also struggled with having a Korean passport and with having grown up in Thailand—both of them being countries people weren't too familiar with."

Despite Grace's perfectly fluent American English that she picked up from her American school in Thailand, she lacked familiarity with American pop culture. She recalled not being accustomed to even the concept of a homogenous pop culture that everyone could refer to.

"I think I also struggled with me sounding American but not being American. People tend to have this social tendency of referring to movies, TV shows, or songs. Say, it's a song reference, and they just kind of expect you to get it.

"I never grew up that way because [back in high school,] all my friends were from everywhere. So, it's not just one American movie or one American song. We're listening to different songs, different movies; we talk about cultural things, not like the celebrity culture or pop culture. I think it was just in college when I was like, 'who am I?'"

After struggling to adapt to her new environment as a seventeen-year-old TCT, Grace reached a point where she considered transferring to a different college. Luckily, although she was across the ocean from her old home, she was still in touch with her high school guidance counselor.

"I told my guidance counselor I'm transitioning, and this is really hard. I just can't handle this. I have friends, but they feel shallow. They don't understand me. And then she told me, 'You're not the only one who's going through this right now. All your other friends, even your American friends, are all going through a transition of living with someone they don't know and of taking classes in college.'"

"I think that really was like a wake-up call to me. I'm not the only one who's struggling."

After that, Grace slowly grew attached to her college community. She was actively involved with the campus community and even worked as an RA for a couple of years.

This did not necessarily mean that everything worked out afterward. Graduating and making choices for herself was still a continuous struggle—especially as an ATCK.

"The world is my oyster. I think it really is. But there are too many options. I think as a TCK, or just as a person with high expectations, I want excellence and I want the best. So, as an adult, it's harder to make decisions, because I'm always thinking, 'What are the repercussions of living in this country? If I go there, what am I missing out on?'

"There are just way too many thoughts involved. Whereas when I was a kid, I just didn't know much. Knowledge is power, but ignorance is definitely bliss."

"Now that I'm an adult, I know more. I'm responsible for all my stuff. Moving is hard because of visas. I have to think about buying tickets on my own, setting up on my own, settling in my house on my own, and making connections on my own. I have so much more responsibility than I had when I was a kid."

Grace's words really capture the "adulting" involved with being a TCT. For all their lives, TCTs have had choices made *for them.* They did not choose to live outside their passport country. Their parents, their parents' bosses, the government, or someone else always made important life decisions for them. Once they grow up and have to make decisions on their own, they can feel extremely overwhelmed. This is worsened by their international backgrounds and talents. They not only have the option to work where they live but also to use their multicultural background to go beyond—to anywhere in the globe. That's a lot to think about!

But at times of such uncertainty, Grace is glad that she has mentors and friends to rely on from all over the world.

"To teens in college, enjoy college. And it's okay to have questions. And it's okay to not have life figured out. First of all, get a mentor. Find someone that you really respect that you can go to on a weekly or biweekly basis, ask questions. Find the people that will be your lifelong friends. There are friends who are just for a season, but there are also friends who are there for life."

Her second advice pertained to making memories. For Grace, wherever she is in the world, her memories are what comforts her the most.

"Really try to make good, quality memories and be kind to other people. Because your home may change and your high school campus may change, and the teachers may change, but that spirit will still be there. That's what remains. And that's what you want to come back to. In a world that's constantly changing around you, that's the thing that remains the same."

As I left the campus after the interview and looked back upon my somewhat unfamiliar campus building, I realized what Grace meant.

Even if one day I may not even get the opportunity to return to Qingdao—let alone my high school building—the friends I've made and the memories I've made there will always remain in my heart.

I, hence, forever have a home in my heart.

# CHAPTER 5:

# TECHNOLOGY

———

*"I realized it's not worth the effort when clearly what that friendship needs is an in-person contact."*

— LINDIE BOTES

I have a friend in Slovenia whom I have not met in person in almost three years. But we frequently talk through Facebook Messenger—or we used to.

The messenger used to be pretty active for the first couple of months after our in-person encounter. As both of our lives started to get busier, the frequency of those messages died out.

That did not mean, however, that we did not update each other on our lives. We have instead resorted to sending each other extremely long messages with dozens of pictures every couple of days.

I would say our relationship lies in the middle ground of a classic "pen pal" and immediate, physical friendship.

We are traditional "pen pal" friends in that we will probably not be seeing each other in person in years, almost to the point where we might just be strangers. We update each other on our lives because we live such different lives, and we find those differences interesting.

At the same time, while old pen pal letters back in the day used to take months to deliver, messages only take a second. She is constantly on my feed and knows when I'm online. We both know the details of each other's daily lives.

We live in a truly fascinating time for human connection—all thanks to the internet.

Ever since its invention, the internet has quickly developed into a gigantic web that connects everyone across the globe. Today, finding a single teen on the subway or the elevator who is not on their phone is difficult. The image of teens constantly on their phones has become such a common epidemic that it is not even a joke anymore.

Divided debates persist on whether the internet is beneficial or harmful to teenagers. While many scholars in the past have argued that online relationships are futile and lead to more loneliness, many more modern studies have proven that the internet can be an effective way to form and maintain relationships.[18,19]

---

18    Kimberly S. Young and Robert C. Rogers, "The Relationship Between Depression and Internet Addiction," *CyberPsychology & Behavior* 1, no. 1 (1998): 25.

19    Malinda Desjarlais and Jessica J. Joseph, "Socially Interactive and Passive Technologies Enhance Friendship Quality: An Investigation of the

In this chapter, we'll be exploring both the benefits and burdens that come with the internet—specifically for TCTs.

## MAINTAINING OLD RELATIONSHIPS

The internet and its association with human relationships hold an especially complex significance for Third Culture Teens: not only because they are typical teens obsessed with Instagram and Snapchat, but also because the internet is often the only way to connect with their friends and family members.

This obviously comes with benefits for TCTs. Back in the day, leaving a place meant saying goodbye to it forever. You left knowing you would never be able to see most of your friends again for the rest of your life. You left knowing you would never be able to see the street in front of your home or eat your favorite local cuisine.

With the internet, everything has changed. Goodbyes aren't as permanent as they used to be.

Many forms of online communication, ranging from Face-Time to Zoom to Skype, allow you to stay in touch with your old friends as if you have never left. You can virtually travel to your old home with the road view mode on Google Maps. With Amazon or other international delivery systems, you can order your favorite local snacks to wherever you are in the world.

Mediating Roles of Online and Offline Self-Disclosure," *Cyberpsychology, Behavior, and Social Networking* 20, no. 5 (2017): 286.

Many young ATCKs and TCTs have shared with me the tremendous role technology has played in their relationships.

For Kawtar, thanks to international calls, meeting old friends almost feels as if she has been meeting them in person.

"I have specific times at least once a month or every two months to connect with friends in different time zones. I'll make sure that I have a phone call with them. I do it mindfully, making sure that it's at a time that works for their time zone."

"When I go back home, I connect with them, I make sure to meet them [in person.]"

Kawtar also notes that the "little things" are what truly keep her connected to her friends.

"And that really helps a lot—just those little things. When it's their birthday or New Year's, I'll make sure to just send the message once in a while. Those little things keep the wind going until we meet again and when we—girlfriends that I've met again after twenty years or so at this point—do meet again, it feels like we've never split up."

Grace, similarly, emphasized the importance of mindfully creating the time to catch up with old friends to maintain former relationships.

"My one close friend in particular, she and I schedule a time to call every two months or so. We maintain our relationship that way. I would say calling, texting, and being intentional about creating space and time to spend quality time with them [is very important]."

As seen above, both Grace and Kawtar base a lot of their former relationships on online means of communication such as calling or messaging.

For Lindie, in fact, the other person's willingness to maintain relationships through means of online communication is a big determinant for her relationships.

"I feel like it's a two-way thing. I had a best friend in university in South Africa and we just stopped talking when I went to Singapore not because the friendship is over, but because we never had that experience of our friendship being in two different countries. Some people don't know how to handle that. For me, that's super normal. I can Skype them every week."

"But for other people who are only friends with people in their neighborhood, if I suddenly move overseas, they are just like, 'It's so much effort and I'm not going to talk to Lindie.' When that happens, I do my best to keep in touch with them and tell them I'm doing okay and miss you and whatever, but I realized it's not worth the effort when clearly what that friendship needs is an in-person contact."

A common factor in all of our interviewees' stories is that in order for former relationships to stay intact, interactions with them have to be *mindful* and *intentional*.

While it sounds easy on paper, we all know making the time in our current lives to consistently stay in touch with those who are not directly a part of our lives anymore is quite difficult.

As Lindie has mentioned, this form of relationship is met with different responses from different people.

Some friendships require constant in-person connection—obviously, this is not the circumstances many TCTs are in. Because of this, many TCTs are cautious when it comes to starting new relationships. Even with the internet, some people just can't make the time to maintain long-distance relationships, and knowing this, TCTs often feel too intimidated to begin a relationship as such in the first place. They know that a goodbye will eventually come.

Other friends will require some form of connection, but to a manageable degree. Kawtar mentioned how sending yearly birthday messages or New Year's messages has helped her maintain her former relationships. Sometimes, all it takes is for you to simply remind them every once in a while that you still care and think about them.

Having formed and dissolved many relationships throughout my life, I truly appreciate friends who do not mind continuing the relationship through such minimal amount of connection. Perhaps because of my appreciation for them, these are the people I have maintained the most intimate relationships with.

The one friend whom I've known for the longest period of my life—since 7th grade when we went to middle school together in Korea until now—is equally as bad at staying in touch with me as I am with her. We rarely send each other messages and meet up barely once every year.

Yet, because we send those annual "happy birthday" and "happy New Year's" messages to each other, I still feel a strong attachment toward her that rekindles within me every time we meet again. Perhaps because of this, (or perhaps because we literally did not change over the years) seeing her today feels the same as seeing her seven years ago.

Our relationship, of course, comes with downsides—we don't know the minor details about each other's lives very much. But we try our best to catch each other up when we do meet in person, which I do not mind doing and actually enjoy very much.

Some people are not like my friend and me. Some friends need to make weekly Skype calls, as Grace does with her friends, or even daily text updates.

As a note, all of the above forms of interactions apply the same way to romantic or familial relationships. Many TCTs struggle with keeping in touch with their distant family members, including cousins, uncles, and others who do not live in the same country as them. For those who moved to another country for college, the same struggle goes toward maintaining relationships with their parents and siblings.

While no one right answer exists to which kind of online interaction is the most ideal, I believe a common understanding on preferred frequency of connection is necessary.

I work well with my friend from Korea because we have a similar tendency of (being too lazy and) not contacting each other very frequently. Yet we still stay in touch because that works for the both of us.

If you yourself require more attention and updates to maintain a friendship, you will have to find a friend who is equally devoted to doing that as much as you are.

This also means that you might have to back down a little to find that common ground. Sometimes, your friend might ask you to contact them more than you had expected to. Other times, you would be disappointed in your friend for not contacting you as frequently as you might have wanted.

Communication is key to such times of conflict. Message them directly about how you are feeling—or even better, call them through FaceTime or Skype. Feelings are often miscommunicated through written words, and the two of you clearly setting out how you want to stay in touch is important.

The good news is that according to studies, mobile technology has generally helped Third Culture Kids practice their social and interpersonal skills. Many TCKs have commented that talking with friends online has helped them "exercise reflexivity to think more freely about who they are and practice acquired cross-cultural skills."[20] So the more opportunity

---

20   Erika Valencia, "Neo-Filipino: A Study on the Impact of Internet and Mobile Technology on the Identity of Selected Filipino Third Culture Kids," (master's thesis, University of Santo Tomas, 2016), 22.

you have to communicate with friends online, the better you will get at interacting with them—both online and in real life.

Online friendships are just like relationships in real life. They require effort, dedication, and empathy.

As Lindie boldly stated, if the other person doesn't want to make the time for you, the relationship is unfortunately just not worth it.

## THE "SCHIZOPHRENIC" EXPERIENCE

Technology brings in additional complexities to the TCT experience. Beyond communicating with individuals is also the issue of culture.

For instance, if you are constantly connecting with people in other countries, how does that influence your experience assimilating into your new environment? Moreover, if all your friends are living in different countries around the world, just how many stories and issues around the world do you have space for in your life?

With the internet, keeping yourself updated with the trends and cultures of a country different from the one you are living in is much easier. If you are constantly surrounding yourself with, for instance, Korean culture from back home while you are living elsewhere, are you really a Third Culture Teen just because you physically live in a different country? If your interests and heart remain in Korea through the internet, wouldn't you culturally identify simply as a Korean?

In academic terms, the phenomenon described above is a "re-centering" of your identity due to the online virtual space. This occurs when an "individual creates such cohesive representations that relate to their core identity and performs these representations or roles to other people."[21]

Put simply, the virtual space of the internet provides additional factors to complicate one's identity—in addition to all the identity crises TCTs are going through already.

Ruth, an ATCK of an older generation, believes that the internet actually made the TCK experience harder.

"I think in a way, internet only complicated things. Before, I was at least in London or Chicago; I only had two places, right? But now, you can go to many places. We can travel more and connect more. I think it is even more confusing *because* you can keep up with your friends who are not with you. I don't think it got easier."

For me, as a TCT of the modern age, I occasionally suffer from information overload in my Facebook feed.

Currently living in the United States, I like seeing news about what's going on in the country I live in. I see constant updates about the American president or another wildfire in California in my feed.

At the same time, I have friends from Hong Kong posting articles about the Hong Kong protests. At the same time,

---

21   Ibid., 10.

I have friends from Korea posting articles about the latest Korean celebrity scandal. At the same time, I have friends from Thailand posting about LGBTQ issues in Thailand.

The best word to describe this confusion would be a feeling of schizophrenia. As much as I would like to know and develop interest in all these different topics from around the world, I have only so much emotional and intellectual capacity when I look over my social media feed. Sometimes all this information overwhelms me, and it gets more difficult to concentrate on the current issues that matter most to me at the moment.

As much as the internet made the TCT experience easier in some sense, it has also complicated it, as "leaving" a place is never really "leaving" anymore. Happy memories and friends are not the only things that follow after you when you leave a place; the emotional baggage and distress follow you as well.

The best solution when you feel overwhelmed or feel as if you are torn apart, different pieces of you scattered across various places around the world, is to simply take a break.

What moms say all the time just might be right in this case.

"Get off your phone!"

## THE TCK COMMUNITY

As much as I have criticized the internet for all the complexities that it has provided for us, I have also benefitted tremendously from the internet. In fact, the internet made this very book you are reading possible. Yes, it provided me with a publisher, yes, it provided me with the tools to write the book, but more importantly than anything else, it connected me with TCKs around the world who have provided invaluable stories that make up this book. Some of the interviewees in the book are friends I have made from TCK Facebook groups.

Besides Facebook groups, numerous other online communities and resources for TCKs are available. I would especially like to mention the online magazine *Denizen*. The magazine features different articles written by TCKs about their lives. Although it is not updated anymore, I highly suggest you check them out!

Ruth Van Reken and David Pollock might be the ones who started the TCK phenomenon through their book, but TCTs today have taken the matter into their own modern hands, creating online communities for TCKs around the world to directly communicate and interact with.

I can't thank the various online TCK communities enough for all the support that I have received for writing this book, and I highly encourage any other TCTs to check these online communities out. You can find more information about the websites introduced above and other online sources in the "Additional Resources" section at the end of the book.

Returning to my introduction about the term TCK, the entire point of such a term is so that we feel understood and supported. You might not have a fellow TCT near you, but you can meet and connect with millions of TCTs online. For all the complexities that the internet has cursed us with, it provided us the most convenient ways possible to get to know each other.

So, what are you waiting for? Let's connect!

---

## THREE POINT SUMMARY

- The internet can be used to maintain old relationships—but you have to be intentional with your efforts to maintain them.
- The internet also comes with what I call a "schizophrenic" experience of being bombarded with too much information from around the world.
- Yet, the internet also provides us with a tool to form online TCK communities, connecting TCKs from around the world.

# PART 3:

# THE LIFE WE ARE LIVING

# CHAPTER 6:

# TRANSITIONING & ADULTING

———

*"Okay, then you set the example. . . You model the kind of relationship that you want, and people will respond to that."*

— RACHEL JONES

Most of my school years were spent in a pseudo-American fantasy.

Or, in simpler terms, an American international school.

This meant a majority of my teachers were American, the textbooks that I learned from were American, and the relevant pop culture references between our peers were based on American movie stars and singers. This is all despite the fact that most of my peers were either not American or an American who lived away from the United States for so long they didn't identify as one. And I fit perfectly into this pseudo-American society. In fact, I came to believe that America was *the* place for me—land of diversity, land of democracy, and land of Taylor Swift (yes, I was a huge fan for way too long).

My pseudo-American dream did, in fact, lead me to America. All the colleges I applied to were in the States and my final choice boiled down to either a liberal arts college in Massachusetts or a private university in Los Angeles. I chose LA not only because it was the best place to fulfill my dream as a filmmaker, but also because I wanted to experience American diversity for myself.

What I did not know was that the immediate group of friends I was introduced to at school was far from "diversity." During my first week of school, I realized that "diversity" meant fifteen different cities in the Bay Area—or occasionally Orange County. (Of course, spending more time at school and getting to know more people proved otherwise. In fact, I am blessed to be in one of the most diverse college campuses in America—but even still!) This was especially true for our honors college community that moved in a couple of days earlier than the rest of the freshman cohort.

I still remember our first residential "hangout" session on the lawn late at night. I joined a group of girls only to find out I *literally* had nothing in common with them. Four out of five of them were from the Bay Area. Taylor Swift was no longer relevant in college culture (but electro beat mumble rap hip hop was). Real American high school life sounded nothing like our American international schools. I did not speak a single word during our conversation that night. My cultural background, which I was proud to share in all my previous American international schools, only seemed like a larger divider between everyone else and me.

A sudden feeling of fear swept over me: was I to be forever alone, mute and deaf in every conversation? I thought I *belonged* here, but I had never felt more out of place.

The more scared I got, the more I went out to club events and parties. I became a passive listener rather than a talker. Not to say that listening is in no way less valuable than talking, but my passive listening was out of a genuine fear of sharing about myself. All my small talk consisted of my listening to the other person, vehemently nodding my head to everything they mentioned so I could come off as if I understood everything they were talking about.

I would nod to a reference from *The Office*, nod to Cardi B, and nod to problems with the Democratic Party.

No speaking was involved, but every little nod was a lie about myself. I eventually reached a breaking point, and for an entire week I could not step out of my dorm room except for classes. My tower of little lies was crushing me down; sharing conversations with others almost felt torturous. I was afraid of my lies falling apart with one wrong answer. I was afraid of them leading to people turning away from me. I was afraid that I might end up all alone in a foreign country. This fear was what ironically led me away from meeting people; I wanted all my relationships to remain at a stage in which people found me relevant and interesting. I didn't want to ruin that by attempting to dive into any deeper conversations about my interests and my life story.

One day, I finally broke down in front of my mom on our FaceTime chat. She was surprised and heartbroken, knowing that I had dreamed of coming to the United States for so long. She was so sure, more than anyone else, that I would do great there. Yet here I was, bawling on the phone, admitting to her that I was afraid to go out and meet people. I couldn't relate to anyone. I was different.

I cried out my blatantly obvious yet ironically surprising revelation: "I'm a foreigner here."

Not a lot of things about me have changed from my first week of college. (Except the fact that I now watch *The Office*. I'm on Season 6). I do, however, have friends I can turn to and found a lifestyle that works best for me (I soon discovered that I'm not that into partying). But moreover, none of the friendships I desperately tried to maintain from that first week of college are relevant in my life anymore.

It just never worked out.

Above is the story of my first week at college. It was my first attempt at "adulting."

**ADULTING | ə'DəLTING | NOUN**

The practice of behaving in a way characteristic of a responsible adult.[22]

While many people like to name getting your taxes in for the first time or cooking your first proper meal as evidence of adulting, I want to focus on the social aspects of "adulting" in this chapter.

This is especially pertinent to TCTs, as many of them go "abroad" for college—away from the comforting homes of their expat/multicultural environment and their friends and family for the very first time. As I have discussed earlier in the introduction, the true significance of the term "TCK" never hit me until I was at college in the US—that was the time when a true identity crisis hit me, and I felt the desperate need to define myself.

What does it mean to grow out of the comforts of your expat community and your family?

What does it take to stand on your own as a TCT?

Here's the (un)official adulting guide for TCTs. Note that a lot of it focuses on the college experience (as many TCTs go "abroad" for college), but the same principles apply to any other form of new life you have started on your own as a semi-adult.

---

22   Oxford, "Definition of adulting in English," LEXICO powered by Oxford, accessed 21 February 2020.

This guide will be organized based on Lauren Purnell and Elizabeth Hoban's study, which was, in turn, based on David Pollock's transition model.

In this study, Purnell and Hoban analyzed twelve in-depth interviews with Australian TCKs aged eighteen to twenty-seven years old who had spent three to eighteen years living in different parts of the world including Africa, Europe, and Asia. They all come from various backgrounds, some of them transitioning back to Australia with their family while others came alone, and some of them having lived abroad in a missionary family while others went abroad for educational or business purposes.[23]

According to Pollock's transition model, Third Culture Kids go through five stages when they experience significant transitions in their lives.

The first stage is **involvement**. The TCK feels a sense of commitment and belonging to their current community.

The second stage is **leaving**. The TCK experiences anticipation for their departure and starts to distance themselves from their friends and family.

The third stage is the **crisis phase**. The TCK experiences a sense of anxiety and chaos as everything in their lives is changing.

---

23   Laura Purnell and Elizabeth Hoban, "The lived experiences of Third Culture Kids transitioning into university life in Australia," *International Journal of Intercultural Relations* 41 (2014): 82.

The fourth stage is **entering**. The TCK experiences isolation and vulnerability as a result of uncertainty in their lives.

The final stage is **reinvolvement** as the TCK successfully experiences inclusion in a new location.[24]

Purnell and Hoban have, through their analysis, modified Pollock's model and summarized the four stages of transition that Australian TCKs—or TCTs—experienced throughout their readjustment phase in their Australian universities after their life outside of Australia.

## 1. PREPARATION FOR TRANSITION

The first stage is preparation for transition. This stage refers to the time from when the TCKs prepare to move to when they leave their current host country. According to the study, more than half of the participants dreaded leaving their host country to attend university in Australia.[25] A majority of them reported that they experienced immense stress during this period.[26] Eight of the twelve participants received transition seminars in their high schools but were still unaware of what specific issues they would face.[27]

Just as the eight participants attested, as hard as schools try to prepare you for university life, high school seminars will never be enough to completely capture upcoming college life.

---

24 Ibid.

25 Ibid., 83.

26 Ibid.

27 Ibid.

This is especially true if the education system of the college you are planning to attend does not coincide with your high school's education system. For instance, a common problem found in the study was that many of the Australia-born TCTs went to American international schools when they were living outside Australia.[28] Hence, the teachers there were not fully aware of how college life in Australia would be.

I recommend that in order to fully prepare for your transition into college, you should research as much as you possibly can.

Research what, you ask?

First of all, your favorite hometown food restaurants. No, I'm not joking. I was lucky that Los Angeles, where I go to college, has such a diversity of communities that I had an easy time finding Korean food when I wanted or Chinese food when I wanted. Perhaps for other places in the world, this might not be an option. Look for where the closest restaurants and supermarkets are—you won't believe how much comfort a bowl of familiar food can bring to you on a lonely night.

Now that you have your food emergency kit down, research the culture of the new college/ place of residence you are going to. Watch American television shows if you are going to the US for college for the first time. Watch YouTube vloggers who are already attending your college—especially those "day in a life" videos. Get a sense of how they speak, the activities they do for fun, and how classes are.

---

28  Ibid., 84.

Finally, get the complicated document stuff out of the way. Make sure you get your visa! Many TCTs forget that moving abroad involves signing a lot of documents. Your parents will no longer be doing this for you. Make sure you bring your immigration documents, prepare for your visa, and pay your school fees. If you are planning to get a license in a new country or are looking into renting an apartment to live in, get those things done early so you don't have to be caught up in administrative work in your first few weeks of school. Try your best to get them out of your way so you can focus instead on making friends and adjusting to your new environment.

There are special seminars and books dedicated to helping TCTs prepare to transition specifically to college.

Although an older book, Tina Quick's *The Global Nomad's Guide to University Transition* is a book completely devoted to tips on how to adjust to college as a TCK. Although this article is a little outdated as well, I also recommend reading the article "Third Culture Kid's Guide to College" in *Denizen*.

Interaction International, an American organization devoted to providing care for TCKs, also hosts Transition Seminars every summer for TCTs transitioning to American colleges. It's a seven-day-long retreat in either Colorado or Georgia that seeks to teach TCKs important skills they need to adjust to college.[29]

---

29  "Older Teens," Interaction International, accessed April 3, 2020.

Regardless of how hard you prepare for transitions, however, they are always going to be difficult—especially if this is your first time moving away from your parents!

But I don't need to tell you—a TCT—that.

You know the struggles of transitioning better than anyone else.

## 2. INITIAL TRANSITION

The second stage is initial transition. This stage refers to the first six months in one's new environment.

Nine out of the twelve participants in the study separated themselves from Australian society due to lack of understanding.[30]

One interviewee commented, "I was so used to things in Laos when I came back. I guess I didn't really talk to people because I felt like they didn't really understand my experience."[31]

Most of the subjects reported that they experienced loneliness and depression.[32] More than half of the subjects reported that they struggled to fit into Australian social networks.[33]

---

30  Laura Purnell and Elizabeth Hoban, "The lived experiences of Third Culture Kids transitioning into university life in Australia," *International Journal of Intercultural Relations* 41 (2014): 84.

31  Ibid.

32  Ibid.

33  Ibid.

One subject commented, "I didn't have anything in common with them. We get on fine in class but obviously I'm trying to make friends because I don't have a social network, but they already have their networks from their high school and their life."[34]

At this second stage, Jessica Kim, a Korea-born TCK who had to move to the United States for the first time for college, recommends that you stay flexible with your interests and your identity.

An extrovert with a bubbly personality, Jessica recalled not being quite herself her freshman year of college in our interview. This is because she could not speak or act first when she was clearly different from everybody else here.

"Now that I'm looking back [to freshman year], I'm realizing how less comfortable I was, and how I felt like a smaller person than I was. This is because I was just watching other people and observing how I'm supposed to act. I was the new kid just wanting to see what's 'cool' and how you're supposed to act in certain situations. I don't like being left out, and I don't like being someone who waits for other people's permission to do certain things."

As she began to make more friends from a variety of backgrounds, however, she realized that her concerns were mostly just in her head. She could have good conversations with friends even though they came from very different backgrounds from her. Through that experience, she realized she

---

34  Ibid.

just might have been overthinking the importance of her identity as a Third Culture Kid.

"I wanted to meet more people who are also Third Culture Kids, so I can relate with them, but at the same time, I realized my cultural identity is only one part of me. Maybe with other people, they can relate to your interest in politics or your interest in specific sports. You might be placing too much importance on your identity. Hold your head high because I never did for my freshman year of college. After that period, I realized I was just like everyone else."

As Jessica has said, many TCTs end up overthinking the fact that they are too different from everybody else. That statement could be somewhat valid, but once you start to obsess over that fact, it becomes difficult to step out of your bubble and attempt to make friends with people around you—just like how I was during my first week of college.

Being the "foreigner" or the "TCT" does not define your entire identity. Even though people around you might not relate to your expat experience, they might connect with you over other interests.

Be open-minded and active in your search for new friends and a new community during your initial transition phase. That, however, does not mean you should sacrifice being yourself. If they don't want you for who you are, you do not need to be friends with them. Someone else out there is waiting to meet you and be your new friend!

## 3. ADAPTATION

The third stage is adaptation, which refers to the first six months to two years in your new environment.[35] In this stage, the interviewees recall focusing more on developing social connections rather than the practicalities of adjusting. Through this process, half of the participants relied on other TCK friends for support.[36]

An interesting issue that emerged for many of the participants was the university alcohol culture. This was especially the case for missionary TCKs (TCKs who went abroad due to their parents' missionary work). They were not used to alcohol and felt uncomfortable overall about university students' frequent alcohol consumption.[37] Even for many of the non-missionary TCKs, they started drinking alcohol earlier in their host country and were not used to the "juvenile" alcohol culture of the university students.[38]

Three of the twelve participants also reported that they continued to experience depression or anxiety throughout the entire the transition and adaptation phase.[39] One participant commented that he visited therapists regularly only to find out that other TCKs in his school were already getting emotional help from therapy. He added that he wished others would have told him how "normal" this was earlier.[40]

---

35  Ibid., 85.
36  Ibid.
37  Ibid.
38  Ibid.
39  Ibid.
40  Ibid.

The results of the study, once again, demonstrate the impor- tance of a TCK community for transitioning TCTs. Even after successfully getting over the practical difficulties of transi- tioning to a new environment, TCTs in college constantly face culture shock that not many others in their college com- munity understand. Although not exactly a TCK group, the international student community at New York University helped Fareeha find comfort in her new college environment.

"I think you just find comfort in people that you relate to and I think people who relate to me are those who experi- enced similar things. . .I have these other amazing friends and people that I've met who are also Third Culture Kids or international students, and when I spend time with them, it just makes me feel grateful. . .I think it's just about being grateful for the people that I have around me now."

You can read more about Fareeha's and other TCKs' stories of finding their own community in Chapter 9.

I would also like to point to the participant's comment about therapy being normal. While many cultures have different views on depression or other forms of mental illnesses, know that needing psychological help during your process of tran- sition is completely normal.

Even if you do not seek professional help, I highly encour- age you to speak to a friend whenever you are going through issues.

This is another surprising barrier that TCTs—and college kids in general—are met with in college. Transitioning from the safe nest of your tight-knit expat community to a larger, more individualistic college community might be a large leap for many TCTs, and they might not initially have the courage to bring up their personal issues to their friends.

Rachel Jones comments on this, revealing that her children's most difficult times as TCTs were their first few months in college.

"My kids' hardest times were when they were sophomores in university in the States. They wanted to have deep conversations pretty quickly, but most university students around them were unable to start meaningful conversations, so that's been their biggest challenge."

"My daughter would say the kids at her dorm don't want to have meaningful conversations. I told her, 'Okay, then you set the example. . .You model the kind of relationship that you want, and people will respond to that. People who respond to that would be the ones who will start the relationship with you.'"

"We just encouraged her to be really brave because other kids probably feel isolated as well. It's really important to set an example and to be brave and vulnerable."

TCTs often resort to putting themselves "second" in relationships with others. Because we don't know the "norm" of how other people generally act, we like to stay back and observe before taking action ourselves. Due to our naturally independent nature from years of transitioning between cultures on our own, it becomes even more difficult for TCTs to open up and start deeper conversations with those around them.

Yet, as Rachel shares, setting the example of the relationship you want and being proactive about your relationships is important—especially in the adaptation phase since you now have a somewhat-established network of connections in your life. Now you get to decide what you want to do with the people in your life. This will determine what the rest of your life in your new environment looks like.

You have the power to decide your life and your relationships! Open up to the people around you and seek out the community you need to fully adapt.

## 4. STABILIZATION
The final stage of transition is stabilization.

Purnell and Hoban reported that only half of the twelve participants entered this final stage after being in Australia for two years.[41] Others are still in the third stage. Even among the six who are now in the stabilization phase—feeling practically and socially settled in Australia—four of them commented that they would still like to return to their host country instead of settling in Australia.[42]

The biggest takeaway from the result of the study above is that still feeling uncomfortable and unadjusted in your new college environment is *completely normal.* Half of the study's participants, even after two full years of being in college, did not feel like they have fully adapted to the environment

41  Ibid., 86.

42  Ibid.

around them. Take your time and do not push yourself too hard. Taking a long time to get adjusted to a new environment is only normal—especially for the first time as a semi-adult.

College is hard enough for monocultural teens who left home for the first time. It is even harder for TCTs, as they often are, again, in an entirely new environment and trying to adjust to it entirely on their own.

Accept the feelings within you and seek help if you need to. And if you never fully enter the stabilization phase, you have a whole future ahead of you to decide whether to stay in or leave the community you are a part of right now.

We TCTs are amazing enough for making it this far on our own!

## THREE POINT SUMMARY

- Before your transition, make sure you are prepared for the new environment. Research before you go and get the necessary documents ready and complete beforehand.
- Know that the TCK identity is not everything to who you are. Find other similarities to connect with other people.
- Accept yourself for who you are and be proactive about what you prefer in relationships. You have the right to do that!

# CHAPTER 7:

# THE FEELING OF REALLY UNBELONGING

———

The last time I was most ashamed of myself was when I was watching television with my mom.

We were watching the Korean news, in which a Korean-American man who used to be a singer in Korea back in the early nineties was featured. He debuted as a singer back in the day, but the majority of the conservative Korean public back then did not like how he could not speak fluent Korean. He never found success in Korea and was forced to move back to the United States.

This year, due to younger people's discoveries of his old videos on YouTube, he became a big deal again and was returning to Korea to work as a singer again in his fifties. This man was my mom's biggest interest in these days. She'd been watching every television show and YouTube video featuring him religiously.

My mom was expecting me to praise him for his American ways and his suave and confident un-Korean mannerisms. But instead, I spat back at the television bitterly,

"So he just gets to enter Korea and work there whenever he wants? When he's technically a *foreigner?*"

My mom looked back at me in surprise.

"Since when did you start saying things like this? You of all people."

I retracted remorsefully. I have always argued for more open immigration laws and a more accepting culture for foreigners. I should know this best, and I should care for this most because I have lived as a foreigner for more than half of my lifetime.

Reflecting back upon what experiences made me so bitter, I cannot help but attribute it to feeling like I *really don't belong* somewhere for the very first time.

Under the wings of my parents, living abroad just always felt right, even if the fact that we were not citizens of that country was blatantly obvious.

I was sheltered from the complicated process of getting visas, and our family has always moved due to my dad's job, so we always had a good reason to be there.

I was also sheltered from the discrimination that my parents had to face. My mom says she still cannot forget the day that she and my dad were forced to pay hospital bills for a man my dad accidentally "touched" with our car in China. The man was only really standing next to the car when my dad was driving through the narrow street. The man, however, yelped in pain, and upon realizing that my parents were not Chinese, started to claim that he had broken his leg and had to go through major surgeries. My parents had to wait for his results in the hospital for the rest of the day. They knew that nothing was really wrong with the man. He was taking advantage of the fact that my parents were foreigners to have them pay him.

I was not aware of any of this growing up. Without all the difficult issues like visas, getting a job, or discrimination, living in a foreign country was always just nice and fun.

Coming to college in the United States meant I suddenly had to face all these things on my own.

When I decided to go to college, I had to go to Korea on my own to visit the American Embassy to get my visa. I remember standing in line for three hours, watching the nervous faces of fellow Koreans who desperately wanted their acceptance into this country.

I was interviewed behind a glass wall. Chatters of nervous conversations filled the gray-walled room. Even though I knew that I was most likely to get the visa since I already got accepted to college in the United States, I remember biting my lips in nervousness. I never had to wait for approval to enter a country before. When I was little, my parents "magically" had all the documents prepared—all we needed to do was to go to the airport and *poof!* we were gone. Now, I had to *earn* my spot to pass the border. With a simple mark of a stamp, I could be rejected from entering the country.

Living in America on my own also meant taking care of my own immigration documents. This involves carrying around my I-20 document wherever I go.

I still remember the time I was heading to Portland from Vancouver on the train. I had wrongly assumed that I wouldn't need the immigration document for a train ride (*never ever forget your I-20*), and the immigration officers stopped me from entering the platform.

My train was about to leave, and I was getting desperate—almost breaking down. The man who was checking my documents felt bad for me and told me he would let me pass this one time. The woman next to him clicked her tongue disapprovingly and said, "I would have *never* let you pass. If you want to live in this country, you need to have the responsibility to do so."

Though the feeling of gratefulness washed over me as I boarded the train, the woman's voice kept ringing in my ears.

I have to earn the responsibility to be here.

I realized living in a new country on my own came with new responsibilities. I reflected back upon my parents and wondered just how much responsibility they had to carry to keep all of us safe when I couldn't even remember to carry a two-page paper and almost got deported.

All of this, in addition to the fact that getting internships and jobs as an international student is so much harder, has apparently built up some kind of self-reproach, self-accusation, and some need to be rewarded for my *one* nationality. That is what led me to make such a comment upon witnessing this foreign man who could easily just transition back into Korea.

While I was lost in thoughts, my mom hugged me and said,

"I want you to be successful enough to go wherever you go whenever you want to."

I looked into her eyes and realized that she must have gone through all these ugly feelings while living outside her country for the first time as well—and she was responsible for a whole family, not just herself.

Yet, she was still the most loving and accepting person I knew.

I nodded, and we continued watching television together.

# CHAPTER 8:

# DEALING WITH DIFFERENCES

———

*"In a world that's really divided by prejudice,
TCKs are the best ambassadors for peace."*

— KAWTAR EL ALAOUI

If the title of this chapter is making you go, "Wait, I'm an expert on dealing with differences, I don't need any more lessons on this," that was exactly how I felt when I was leaving my home in China to go to college in the United States.

I grew up in three different countries, crossing between those three countries back and forth for over a decade. I've interacted with people of different cultures and have had a long history of attempting to fit in. I'm an expert on dealing with differences—or so I thought.

I had a very lucky childhood in that I was sheltered from a lot of the more serious issues other TCKs might face in their lives. Many other TCKs suffer serious mental health issues as a result of their life abroad. TCKs brought up in difficult environments with "incidences of violent crimes, kidnapping or political unrest," for instance, are often at risk of post-traumatic stress disorder.[43]

As difficult as interacting with a new culture was at first, I had a relatively easy time adjusting to different environments because I had my family around to guide me through the process. I had a moral compass to tell me when I was right in accepting ideas and when I was not.

Going to college and having to face prejudices and making moral and, at times, political decisions *on my own* was an entirely new challenge for me. It almost felt like *I* was escaping a cultural bubble of my own—the expatriate, TCK bubble. I have had to face many American classmates who were monocultural and did not understand the perspectives of foreigners, let alone expats/TCTs.

Disclaimer warning: the purpose of this chapter is not to disparage or criticize any group of people in particular. I'm not trying to make a moral statement about who is right or wrong or which culture is right and which culture isn't. Instead, I am digging into the very complexity of the cultural and political gray areas that we face as TCTs.

---

43    Kate Mayberry, "Third Culture Kids: Citizens of everywhere and nowhere," *BBC,* November 19, 2016.

I hope that my stories can act as food for thought or a source of comfort for anyone who has felt alone in dealing with similar situations.

## THE ISSUES

### XENOPHOBIA

The coronavirus hit Wuhan, China only a week ago (this was noted December 2019).

My family and I weren't alarmed by it much at first, believing the virus would be limited to the city of Wuhan, but as death counts started to go up and my sister's school got canceled for an additional week, we realized the severity of the situation.

My mom's first impulse was to stay at home when she realized how deadly the virus was. None of my family members stepped out of the house for an entire week. Even when my sister got calls from her friends telling her that they were moving back to their home country, my mom refused to leave.

"This is our home, and we are going to be safe at home."

Meanwhile, my sister's friends, especially those returning to Korea, were met with hostility. All over the news were hateful comments about people coming from China.

First, I saw racist comments about Chinese people and their culture. Awfully hateful remarks about how Chinese people eating disease-inducing animals is "primitive" flooded the news.

Once virus-infected people started to enter Korea, the hostility became even worse—they also started rejecting the entrance of Korean people living in China into Korea. People started online petitions to cancel airlines going between China and Korea. Korean people in the city of Wuhan, safely transported back to Korea by the government's private jet, were refused by cities all over Korea. No city wanted to let those people near them—even though each and every person from the jet was checked by the health administrative officials from the country.

"It's *your* fault for moving to China," they said.

"You *deserve* it."

At this point, even Koreans trying to visit Korea have to enter a raffle to get a plane ticket back to their home country (this has gotten much better now that the situation got better). When the death toll increased by forty this morning, my mom finally changed her mind. She was getting the fastest ticket out of there, and my family *luckily* got a seat on the plane to head back. They had to leave everything behind completely out of the blue—my sister's school, our home, and even our dog left in the vet—but that wasn't the problem. My sister was worried about something else.

"What if people realize I live in China?" she asked me in our FaceTime call.

This is not only a case in Korea. As Robert Fullilove of Columbia University reported to NBC, "Xenophobia will rise in significance to precisely the degree to which our sources of information—all of them, not just media—give us stuff to panic about . . . more panic, more temptation to blame the outsider—the other."[44]

Radio personality Rush Limbaugh advocated for a ban on Chinese passengers being permitted into the United States, and social media started spreading the term "ChiCom virus" to refer to the Chinese Communist government.[45]

I found Fullilove's comment especially interesting. If more panic leads to more temptation to blame the "outsider," what do we TCKs become?

We are outsiders on both ends.

The people in my family are foreigners in China and are hence provided with limited proper health care and information from the Chinese government. Yet, now, as we are *physically* outside the boundaries of our passport country, we have also become outsiders in Korea as well.

It almost seems as if each country is a small circle filled with people, and as soon as you step out of the circle, you are no longer part of the tight group of people within the circle.

You come from outside our circle. You are responsible for that. We don't want you back.

---

44  Julian Shen-Berro and Kimmy Yan, "As Coronavirus Spreads, so does Concern over Xenophobia," NBC News, 29 January 2020.

45  Ibid.

Yet, as our family is going through painful measures in times as such, I cringe as my college friends joke about the coronavirus. Some students started a petition online, demanding to cancel school because of the virus. The top comment, however, was a playful response to the outbreak, reading something like, "I just want to be able to make it to the frat party this weekend."

We say we live in a connected world. It's true. News about the virus spread to media all over the world in just a few hours.

Yet, how connected *are* we in our empathy to the pains of others? At a time of crisis, people immediately turn their back against foreigners, immigrants, and even people from their own country living outside of the country's physical territory.

Why is hate so easy to spread and empathy is not? If information is readily available, yet racist stereotypes and xenophobia persist, does real connection even exist?

These are questions we, as TCTs, constantly have to grapple with, because it directly pertains to our lives. In this difficult time, it even directly pertains to our survival. Sometimes the feeling of unbelonging comes as a physical danger to us—as in the case of my family.


## PATRIOTISM & NATIONALISM

I don't quite remember the details of who, when, where, or why, but I remember one night in college (this is, University of Southern California, or USC for short) when I was surrounded by a group of Korean-American kids. They had all spent their summer in Seoul, Korea together and were showing off about their time at a nightclub.

"When the beat dropped, we started yelling 'USA, USA, USA.'"

I grimaced. I told myself that I misheard them.

"What? You started yelling 'USC?'"

"No, we started yelling 'USA.'"

Of course I didn't mishear them.

"Why?"

Awkward silence filled the room. As always, I was the only non-American in the room. One of the boys perked up defensively.

"Because it's funny."

I remember going back that night and just feeling really mad. I was mad at them for doing something so stupid in someone else's country. I was mad at myself for not questioning them any further. Then I was madder at myself for feeling like I should be the defender of Korea when I was not an "authentic Korean" myself.

In fact, I was bullied in middle school for being a "traitor" to my country at the international school I went to in China. Our science class consisted mostly of Korean classmates, and they were speaking Korean together in a group before class started. They were talking about something offensive the Japanese prime minister had said about Koreans and were going on to make dangerously racist comments about Japanese people.

"You never know if they're talking behind your back."

"Those people always lie about their imperialist history. They can lie about anything."

I listened in silence until derogatory terms started coming up in the mouths of my Korean friends.

"Monkeys."

"Deserve to go *extinct.*"

I stood up.

"I don't think it's right to say those things." I told them. "You can't make sweeping comments about a whole country like that."

One of the kids stood back up to me and gave me a long look.

"You're a *traitor* to your country."

Ever since that day, I was bullied by my Korean classmates for the rest of the year for being a "traitor." All of my friends refused to sit next to me, and I was never again included in any of their conversations.

After that traumatic experience, I had two opposing feelings grow within me. I hated Korean people for thinking I was a traitor. But I also hated myself for being the traitor. Even today, I still feel ambivalent when it comes to the ongoing issue of the Korea-Japan political animosity. Reflecting back on Korea's painful history of imperialism and the Japanese government's refusal to apologize makes me extremely mad. Yet, I just don't think I get as emotionally provoked as a lot of my friends in Korea do.

I have also growingly noticed that I feel some kind of allegiance to China as well—the country I call home at the moment. I absolutely hate it whenever Koreans or Americans make degrading comments about Chinese people. I hate seeing people from English-speaking countries not even attempt to make an effort to speak Chinese to local people in my city. They don't even *try* to speak the language of the very country they live in. They speak English, confidently believing people here would be able to understand them. This offends me—yet, I'm not even Chinese.

In *Third Culture Kids: Growing Up Among Worlds,* Ruth tells the story of Maya, who was born in Russia but moved to the United States when she was sixteen. Being stuck between these two opposing countries, Maya had to constantly deal with a similar culture shock.

"When a friend shares their criticism of the political situation in Russia or a social or cultural aspect, I may agree with the criticism completely, but I still feel offended. . . My divided loyalty is rooted in feeling tied to both countries by deep life experiences that are hard to separate from specific instances."[46]

Divided loyalty, moreover, came with divided indifference for Maya.

"The feeling of 'why should I care? Rhis is not really my culture' . . . the indifference sometimes creeps up when feeling particularly torn."[47]

TCTs, especially those in delicate global situations like Maya is in, have to carry on the guilt of their lack of patriotism or their excess of allegiance to their home countries. This often eats them up inside as they are constantly judged and criticized by those from either country.

The dilemma continues when it comes to the issue of not just politics between countries but broader value systems.

Being raised in the Western education system, I have always had a more "liberal" point of view when it came to issues of equality between genders. This led me to always look at my own Asian culture with discontent, and I had come to believe that I would never fully adapt to contemporary Korean society.

---

46  David C. Pollock, Ruth E. Van Reken, and Michael V. Pollock, *Third Culture Kids: Growing Up Among Worlds* (Boston: Nicholas Brealey Publishing, 2010), 142.

47  Ibid.

Yet learning about third world feminist theories in class made me reassess whether I, just like the English speakers in China, was imposing a Western perspective on my own country.

How much freedom is actually free? Is imposing the look of this "woman freed by feminism" actual systemic freedom? How does this concept play into a whole different country established upon a different societal and cultural context? Or am I simply asking these questions because I cannot break out of my "conservative" Asian mindset myself?

Questions as such have become legitimate research topics in the interculturalist academia.

In her article, scholar Danau Tanu specifically discusses the effect of "global education" on TCKs from Asia.

"In the case of TCKs from Asia, how does an 'international education' based on Western liberal-humanism affect their identity? Do they become 'genuinely' cross-cultural, or do they espouse a cultural hierarchy in their absorption of Western culture?"[48]

I still do not have the answers to the questions above.

Walking the tightrope between Korea, China, Malaysia, and the US and between "Eastern" and "Western" value systems will forever be a task I am destined to embark on.

---

48   Danau Tanu, "Global Nomads: Towards a Study of 'Asian' Third Culture Kids," *Conference: 17th Biennial Conference of the Asian Studies Association of Australia, At Melbourne* (2008).

## PREJUDICE

Anyone who's remotely interested in Korean food has been to this restaurant in Koreatown in Los Angeles: Sun Nong Dan.

Famous for its beef broth soup and barbecue, the place is always flooded with various customers. Some are Korean Americans from the neighborhood coming for a taste of authentic Korean food, others are those who have grown an interest in Korean cuisine, and surprisingly many are Chinese international students from nearby colleges missing a nice old Asian-style soup to soothe their stomachs.

The servers there have an extremely perceptive eye from years of dealing with these different kinds of customers. The moment they read the customer's name out loud on the reservation list outside the door and meet eyes with the hungry customer who perks up at the sound of their name, they know which language to use and what attitude to treat the customer with.

If the customer looks Korean, they speak quickly in Korean, expecting them to make a quick choice from the menu. If the customer is a non-Korean, they speak in English and are a little more patient with them. They take the order not using the name of the dish, but in the number associated with that dish on them menu.

For some reason, I always end up visiting Sun Nong Dan with my Chinese friends. That one night, I also went with my Chinese friend who reserved the place with her English name.

With a quick perceptive look at me and my friend, the server made his decision: non-Korean. He asked us to choose from the menu in English, and we accordingly answered him the English way: "number two and number seven please."

After fifteen hungry minutes, we finally got to take a seat in the restaurant. I eagerly reached for the plate of kimchi, my favorite part of the meal. Unfortunately, the kimchi plate was empty. I instinctively held up my hand to call the server—classic impatient Korean way, we never wait for the server to come to *us*—and asked in Korean, "Can you give us more kimchi please?"

The server nodded but looked a little taken aback. He laughed as he told me, "I didn't know you're Korean. You tricked me."

Obviously, he meant it as a joke or maybe a kind of humorous apology for wrongly assuming I was not Korean. But that comment stuck with me for the entire night.

"Am I tricking people by my appearance and my behavior?"

The way he used the word "trick" conjured up a sense of guilt within myself. I never meant to trick anyone. I never meant to pretend to be something else.

Since then, I always made my Korean identity intentionally clear whenever I interacted with Korean people in Koreatown. Before they even spoke to me, I would order food in Korean. Sometimes I'd intentionally read out the names of the menu to my friend, so that others know that I'm Korean.

One day, I was riding back home in an Uber from Koreatown. The driver was Korean-American. As soon as she spotted my obviously Korean name, she started telling me stories about all the famous actors she knows in Korea.

"You know so-and-so, right? My friend here is a friend of him."

I remained quiet.

"Don't tell me you haven't heard of him?"

I shook my head. Not having grown up in Korea, I wasn't an expert in Korean pop culture.

Her elated face quickly darkened, and the rest of the ride was quiet. In that awkward silence, I, again, felt like an imposter. This time, for looking like a Korean then letting my Uber driver down because I was not Korean enough.

Looking back upon my two experiences in Koreatown, I came to a sad realization that I will always be "tricking" someone in Koreatown.

My obviously Korean name and appearance, in addition to my fluent Korean, give the false appearance that I'm Korean. Yet, my non-Korean behavior and culture give the false appearance that I am merely pretending to be one.

This realization, ironically, gave me the confidence to act however I want to. I speak Korean when I feel like it. I don't if I don't feel like it.

I am no imposter of anything. I'm just me.

In a previous edition of *Third Culture Kids,* David Pollock and Ruth Van Reken align four different ways in which someone can interact with their surrounding culture.

- **Foreigner**: Look different, think different
- **Adopted:** Look different, think alike
- **Hidden Immigrant**: Look alike, think different
- **Mirror**: Look alike, think alike[49]

Being situated in Los Angeles where many Korean immigrants live, I ironically had to deal with the problem of being a *literal* "hidden immigrant." I *look* like a Korean immigrant but am far from being one.

While my case and story are very specific, many other TCTs who had to relocate to their passport country struggle with the prejudices that come with being a Hidden Immigrant. Because they look alike to those around them, others assume—and expect—particular behaviors and beliefs from these TCTs. As discussed, numerous times throughout the book, that is why this "return home" often ends up being the biggest challenge for TCTs.

Their appearance is associated with people's prejudices about them, and TCTs are always faced with the task of justifying and explaining themselves.

---

49   David C. Pollock and Ruth E. Van Reken, *Third Culture Kids: Growing Up Among Worlds* (Boston: Nicholas Brealey Publishing, 2001), 53.

## THE SOLUTION (?)

Above are three separate thought pieces I wrote while getting by as a TCT going to college in Los Angeles.

I had to add a question mark to the word "solution" because I have never gotten myself completely over those issues. Whenever I feel like I have the answers, fear and self-doubt wash over me again, and I'm often left more confused than I was before.

Whenever I have these doubts about myself, I like to think that I have been cursed—but also blessed—with having excess empathy. Having looked beyond national and cultural borders, I easily relate to the perspectives of different groups of people and understand the horrid feeling of being stereotyped or othered within a group of people.

I like to think that the only way to be a "patriot" for me is to become a bridge between different cultures. I'll never be as passionately committed to a single national cause as others, perhaps. But I'll always connect and empathize, and that is a talent I believe can help a country—or really, the whole world—grow in love.

The first step to becoming this bridge is to accept yourself for who you are. You do not ever have to change the way you view yourself because other people see you differently. Only when you are comfortable with asserting your own identity for yourself can you step out to become a helping bridge for other people.

Kawtar put it beautifully for TCTs struggling stuck between cultures.

"My biggest advice will be, give yourself the freedom to discover your true multifaceted identity. Though you are in a unique position for having interacted with so many people, you will likely not fit anyone's mold. Make peace with that. You will always find people who will love the diversity you bring.

"In a world that's really divided by prejudice, TCKs are the best ambassadors for peace. Traveling and living in other cultures forces TCKs to be open to the beauty of diversity. They have lived with people who have very different mindsets. Yet, across these differences, TCKs have learned to build bridges, to connect, to make friends, and see the best in others, who sometimes look, feel, and act in ways that can be completely foreign and disorienting at first.

"We, as a TCK, know how to walk into a room and connect with people from so many different backgrounds. We are in a unique position to create bridges where others are building walls. I think that's really precious in this world. Build your own bridges and extend them to others. Appreciate your own diversity ."

Whatever difficult situation you face out in the world as a TCT, know that this will one day all be an experience to look back upon to help you become a better "ambassador for peace."

I'm sorry: the pain you receive from other people's judgments and prejudices will never go away. But you can use this in turn to empower yourself and your community.

Be confident, be bold, be whoever you define yourself to be.

## THREE POINT SUMMARY

- As a TCT in an American college, I have dealt with issues of xenophobia, patriotism, and prejudices.
- This comes from our blessing/curse of empathy for others.
- Use this to make this world a better place—you can act as a bridge or a "peace ambassador" between different cultures.

## CHAPTER 9:

# FINDING & CREATING A COMMUNITY

---

*"I just think that a little bit of validation, a friendly support network, and advice from older TCKs can make that college transition less overwhelming."*[50]

— STEPH YIU

This is what the movies tell you about going to college and/or growing up: glamorous parties, inspiring mentors and professors, hot guys and/or girls to mingle with, and, most of all, finally figuring your life out.

This is what the movies *don't* tell you: loneliness, depression, self-doubt, and anxiety.

---

50   Steph Yiu, "Not 'coming home' alone," *Denizen for Third Culture Kids*, 6 December 2008.

What's worse is that the unfortunate parts of growing up feel five times worse as a TCT. Most of the time, our parents are not around to visit every weekend. Most of the time, we have difficulty explaining ourselves to other people. Naturally, we are more prone to loneliness or depression.

The only cure to this, ironically, is people. Humans are social animals, and we—whether we like it or not—need other people to get by.

The important part of finding/creating a community for yourself is that you feel comfortable being yourself in that community. A community in which you cannot be yourself is worse than no community at all (refer to my first week of college story in Chapter 5!).

In this chapter, we look into the different communities you can seek or create during your new era of semi-adulthood.


## TCK COMMUNITIES

The TCK community is an important resource for TCTs. Talking and connecting with other TCTs help you realize that you are not alone in your struggles. Many other TCKs have gone through the same problems, and many ATCKs out there are happy to help you through them.

Especially if you are in an area without a lot of TCKs or CCKs, try seeking TCK communities to help you find a group of people you can feel more at ease with.

## CREATING CAMPUS TCK COMMUNITIES

In her 2008 article in *Denizen*, Steph Yiu describes her friend Caleb who committed suicide in college in 2005.

"At Caleb's memorial, his dad read his suicide note. 'I'm sorry,' Caleb wrote. 'I've been living a lie.'"[51]

Caleb was a TCK who was born in America but spent most of his life in Hong Kong.

"Caleb often joked that he was that 'blond kid from Hong Kong,' but it couldn't have been easy, being far away from his family, straddling the worlds of American and Cantonese culture."[52]

Yiu writes that Caleb's struggles in college that led to his death reminded her of how much support Third Culture Kids need when they leave their expatriate communities for the first time.

According to scholar Esther Schubert, TCK suicide rates go up after their first year away from "home."[53] With the pressure of new cultural expectations added to being away

---

51   Ibid.

52   Ibid.

53   Esther Schubert, "Keeping Third-Culture Kids Emotionally Healthy: Depression and Suicide Among Missionary Kids," in *ICMK Compendium: New Directions for Mission: Implications for MK,* ed. Beth A. Tetzel and Patricia Mortenson (Brattleboro: Association of Christian Schools International, 1986), 205.

from their family and friends for the first time, many TCTs experience depression and anxiety as Caleb had.

The problem is support groups specifically made for TCKs are extremely difficult to find at college campuses. This is because the TCK experience has not yet been normalized, and thus schools struggle with identifying TCKs in the first place.

Various colleges, however, have made some efforts to recognize TCKs and provide support for them.

In 2000, Cate Whitcomb, who worked for student affairs at Northwestern University, searched for students that had different countries listed for their nationalities and their permanent addresses. Six years later, she started a TCK group.

"You just cannot make assumptions by looking at people and saying, 'I know who you are and where you're from,'" Cate said in an interview.[54]

"When we reduce each other to what we see, we have nothing."[55]

The TCK group at Northwestern met once a quarter for brunch and shared their "culture shock" stories with each other.

Some campuses even have university-recognized TCK groups.

---

54   Steph Yiu, "Not 'coming home' alone," *Denizen for Third Culture Kids*, 6 December 2008.

55   Ibid.

Lewis & Clark College in Portland, Oregon, for instance, was the first school in the United States to start a TCK group—all the way back in 1992.[56]

According to the Lewis & Clark College website, approximately 140 Third Culture Kids study at Lewis & Clark college each year. The campus Third Culture Kid program provides "TCK Thursdays," biweekly social gatherings of TCKs; "Dinner Trips," group outings to international restaurants in Portland; and a "TCK Symposium," which includes keynotes and panel discussions that specifically focus on topics within the TCK realm.[57]

Eastern Mennonite University in Harrisonburg, Virginia, also has a Third Culture Kids Student Fellowship—a club that offers a place of fellowship and support for TCKs. The club regularly goes on fun activities together and are supported by nearly twenty faculty and staff members who are ATCKs.[58]

Yiu wonders if a TCK support group could have helped Caleb with his struggle back in 2005.

"I'm not saying a TCK group would've made all the difference in Caleb's life and death. And I don't think TCKs should only hang out with other Third Culture Kids—quite the opposite.

56  "Third Culture Kids/Global Nomads," Lewis & Clark College, accessed March 27, 2020.

57  Ibid.

58  "Third Culture Kids Student Fellowship," Eastern Mennonite University, accessed March 27, 2020.

I just think that a little bit of validation, a friendly support network, and advice from older TCKs can make that college transition less overwhelming. Too often TCKs are alone in their repatriation struggle, and in this day and age of globalization, that's just unacceptable."[59]

Being a part of a TCK group may have powerful impacts on you as a TCT in a new campus environment. As Yiu has written, it makes all the difference in the world to have a supportive community in which your pain and struggles can be validated and understood. You can also make new friends who have lived a life similar to yours.

The unfortunate reality is that the concept of Third Culture Kids is not yet normalized in most universities around the world. While most universities do have an international student office, many of them do not specify "TCKs" within the international student body. Accordingly, many of the so-called "domestic students" who are TCKs are left out of the programs these international student offices provide. Pressured to be like the other "domestic students," yet not provided with the guidance of adjusting to their new environment, many of these "domestic" TCKs—such as Caleb from Yiu's story—are oftentimes lost and in need of the most support.

If your university campus does not have a TCK group, I highly encourage you to create one yourself! You might be surprised to find out how many fellow TCTs on your campus are looking for other TCTs as well. You might discover

---

59    Steph Yiu, "Not 'coming home' alone," *Denizen for Third Culture Kids*, December 6, 2008.

a new, dependable family that you did not know existed on campus before.

If you do not belong to a college campus or are looking for TCK communities to join outside of college campuses, many organizations around the world lead seminars and provide support groups specifically designed for TCKs.

Refer to additional resources at the end of the book to discover which organizations might be most helpful for you.

**ONLINE TCK COMMUNITIES**
If seeking and creating TCK communities in real life sounds too overwhelming for you (I'm an introvert—I totally understand), try seeking TCK communities online.

Many Facebook groups, Slack groups, and even KakaoTalk groups have all been specifically created for TCKs to meet and mingle!

I benefitted tremendously from the supportive TCK online groups that I have been a part of. I was surprised to find that although most people in the group were complete strangers—and many of whom I will probably never get to meet as we live in opposite corners of the world—they were only too happy to help me out in my interview and promotion for *The Third Culture Teen*. All of the online communities I am a part of are full of positive energy and support that I'm sure a lot of struggling TCKs out there would benefit from.

Many of them post relatable memes about the expat experience and others share their personal issues and their expat journey. These communities often hold fun group sessions online through Skype or Zoom. Some of them hold local group meetings where members living in the same area can meet up in real life as well.

I especially want to recommend the Citizens of the World Slack group. They provide specific threads for different needs such as #tckwellbeing, and also provide fun online activities such as #guessmylocation (where people post pictures of where they currently are, and others try to guess!).

Again, refer to additional resources at the end of the book for suggestions on online TCK communities.

## NON-TCK COMMUNITIES

At the same time, TCKs are not the only people who can understand and care for you. In fact, a majority of your social circle will consist of non-TCKs.

Here are four TCTs' journeys on finding an accepting community in college.

### THE INTERNATIONAL STUDENT COMMUNITY

A common community in which we find ourselves at home is the international student community in college. While international students may not exactly be Third Culture Teens, they are also going through the same expat experience of studying in a foreign country, providing us with something to relate to.

Here is Fareeha's insight into finding home amongst other international students in college.

Fareeha was born and raised in Dhaka, Bangladesh, until second grade. She then moved to Jakarta, Indonesia, with her family, where she attended an international school. After three years, her family moved to Dubai, UAE, where she continued to attend an international school. After graduating from high school in Dubai, she moved to New York City to attend New York University (NYU).

Only when she moved to an environment where international culture was not the norm, and she was, for the first time, not surrounded by other Third Culture Kids like herself, did her identity as a Third Culture Kid—and an international student—hit her. She delineated the three kinds of students she found during her time at NYU.

"There're generally three types of students: there are domestic students who are American and grew up here, there are international students who grew up in their home country and then came to the US, and then there are international students who are Third Culture Kids. Of course, there're people in between but those are just generally the people that I've met."

When she first came to college, she intentionally pushed herself away from the group of students she felt were similar to her.

"When I actually first got here, I was super against being around people who are similar to me because I had this idea that I'm coming to be exposed to different people and communities. I can't just stick around with other international kids or TCKs or brown people. I pushed myself to actually venture out, and I think when I tried to do that freshman year, I was not happy. I definitely did find some other friends because I pushed myself but NYU, at that point, didn't feel like home."

Only when she accepted her international culture, and found a close group of friends who lived in environments similar to those she lived in, did she finally feel like she was fully open with everyone around her.

"I think you just find comfort in people that you relate to, and I think people who relate to me are those who experienced similar things."

This did not mean she closed herself off from those who were different from her. In fact, finding her close group of friends helped her feel more comfortable with herself. She was able to open herself more fully to others—even those who were different from her—and made friends with "really cool people" around her.

She admits, however, that she had a hard time coming to terms with this side of her.

"Interacting with people just made me realize how much in the middle I am and how difficult it all is. Sometimes I feel like I'm missing out on a community, but also, on the other hand, I have these other amazing friends who are also international students. When I spend time with them, it just makes me feel grateful."

"Like, who cares? I'm not a part of that community, but at least I've got my own, and I think it's just about being grateful for the people that I have around me now."

A journalist at Her Campus Media at NYU and co-program chair of the NYU Islamic Finance group, Fareeha fully embraced the international student culture as her own and is thriving at NYU.

**FINDING FAMILIAR COMMUNITIES**
Finding familiar communities can take different forms than you might have expected. Just because someone looks like you or shares a part of your culture does not mean you will necessarily connect the best with them.

For Kayla Cao, a Chinese Canadian raised in China, the Chinese American Student Association on campus was not the right fit for her, and she failed to connect with the culture of the association.

"I tried to join CASA (Chinese American Student Association), but a lot of them are so different from me. I find it more difficult to connect with them than with my other friends who are not Chinese at all. For some reason, there's such a big gap with my world and their world although we are both Chinese. So, by the end of freshman year, I didn't have any Chinese-American friends."

Instead, she found home in communities that are far different from the culture of her upbringing.

"In freshman year, my closest friends were my roommates. We lived together for a while. I was close with my other suite-mates as well. One's Hispanic and the other was Indian. I also connected with my boyfriend who is half Mexican."

Rachel Jones told a similar story about her white American son raised in East Africa trying to find a community in college in the United States.

"My son goes to school in Wisconsin. He joined the African Student Association, and everybody looked at him like 'What are you doing here?' Once they started talking, he realized most of the other kids in the group grew up in the United States, while my son had spent his whole life in Africa, so he knew the most about the continent."

"Once they realized that, they accepted him into the community and looked beyond just what he looks like. He had to learn how to be intentional and vulnerable about his background, so that people won't just make assumptions."

Sometimes the community you fit into best may not be the community others may presume you might belong in.

For Kayla, although she looks like and shares similar experiences with Chinese Americans, she did not feel comfortable there. She instead felt more comfortable around people who were of completely different cultures from her.

For Rachel's son, although he did not look African and was not welcomed by the association at first, because he learned to be vulnerable and honest with his background, he could find a real home amongst people he felt comfortable with.

The takeaway in both stories is that one has to be, as Rachel phrased it, "intentional and vulnerable" about their background. You should not make judgments based on how other people view you. If you feel comfortable in a certain community, you have the right to stay there and make it your home.

Your home community might come to you in the most unexpected forms. Be open-minded and embrace it!

After all, that's what we're best at.

Regardless of whether you find a home among other TCKs, among other international students, or among an entirely new group of friends, what matters is that you have a community for yourself.

College, and late teen years in general, is a constantly changing time in your life, so having someone to share your feelings with is important.

Be proactive and seek out the people you'd like to spend the rest of your college years—and beyond—with!

## THREE POINT SUMMARY

- You can find a community among other TCTs! Seek your closest TCK community online or on your college campus.
- You can also find a comforting community among international students.
- You can also find a community among an entirely new group of friends! What matters is that you have a reliable, welcoming community of your own.

# PART 4:

# THE LIFE WE WILL LIVE

# CHAPTER 10:

# MAXIMIZING YOUR ADVANTAGES

---

*"[Being a TCK] definitely made me adaptable . . .
that could be a strength and sometimes a
weakness. It also made me empathetic—also
definitely a strength but also a weakness.
It's all about how you use it, right?"*

— AMY MCMILLEN

We have discussed the downsides and struggles of being a TCT (or a TCK). But the truth is, being a TCK also comes with amazing perks. As Amy has wonderfully said above, whether these traits become disadvantages or advantages really depends on how you use them.

Below is a guide to help you first identify and then maximize your advantages as a TCK to the fullest degree.

## 1. KNOWING VARIOUS LANGUAGES AND CULTURES

Being a Third Culture Teen in college, I found it difficult to relate with others on a deeper level. I might find one thing in common with someone else—a singer we both like, a major we are both in, and even a city we are both accustomed to—but beyond that, I had difficulty finding things to discuss. The longer the conversation got, I had to constantly strain to think of another topic to bring up. My life was so different from other people's, such that carrying on meaningful conversations beyond simple introductions was difficult. I struggled to relate to others and others felt the same way about me because the life I've lived was so different from that of most people.

At the same time, the practical benefit of being a TCK is that having small talk and networking with strangers from a diversity of backgrounds is much easier. It comes with not only the explicit fact that you might be able to speak their language but also from cultural or regional references that can make people feel instantly closer to you.

This really hit me one day when I was working as a production assistant at a film shoot in Los Angeles last semester. Being an aspiring filmmaker, I often get asked to work at film shoots.

Film shoots are like most working environments—but much quicker and intense. Lots of conversations need to go around to finish each task every minute of the eight-hour-long shoot for the day. That means even as an assistant, you need to be alert to people's needs and quickly respond to their demands.

This film shoot I was working on that day was a graduate student thesis film. The grad school has many more international students, and most people are not as fluent in English as undergrad students are.

The shoot was directed by a Chinese-American woman, and most of the crew members were Chinese.

When the producer was first explaining technical roles for me in English, she was having a difficult time letting words flow through her mouth. She stuttered a bit and looked extremely frustrated about it because she knew that she had a lot of work to do.

When the day was getting busier, she would tell me the tasks I need to finish, but Chinese would slip out of her mouth because she was in such a rush. When I understood what she meant and replied "copy" back into the talkie, she sounded a little surprised but evidently glad that she did not have to go over the instructions again.

Later in the day, the digital imaging technician (DIT), who is the crew member in charge of keeping track of video files, recognized my Korean name and told me that he was from Korea as well. He also needed extra hands with his work and started instructing me on what to do in Korean.

For the rest of the day, many of the crew members gave me instructions in Chinese, Korean, and English and relied on me more comfortably because they knew they did not have to run things through in their head again in another language. I acted as the bridge between each crew member, interpreting things where needed and providing assistance without much difficulty.

The producer later approached me and told me how much she appreciated my presence at the shoot. I was asked to come work again for the rest of the film shoot and had the privilege to see and experience how bigger film shoots work. The biggest privilege for me as a production assistant (I'm sure a lot of interns and assistants in various industries would relate) was to feel needed, to know that I provided actual contribution to the film shoot and helped it run a little smoother.

The same day, I used my free time to network with the other crew members around me. This included a good friend I made that day, who is also Chinese. During lunchtime, we sat together and talked about how life in the States was different from life in China. We quickly bonded over our equal love for Chinese skewed meat. Today, we are very good friends, and she grew to be one of my life mentors, being a "jiejie" (older sister in Chinese) who already graduated grad school and is also working toward the same goal of becoming a filmmaker. I also became friends with the Korean DIT who, appreciating my work on this film shoot, invited me to work at another film shoot that he directed later that year.

Speaking three languages fluently that day helped me feel more connected to every crew member on the shoot. I realized that all the amazing friends and opportunities that came out of this film shoot would not have been possible if it weren't for my ability to network and communicate with people from different countries.

Coming to college, especially for film school, meant lots of networking and communicating with people I've never met before. I have to admit, as an introvert, that was one of the most difficult parts of college. While I won't understand Korean or Chinese or American culture on a complete level, I still found it extremely helpful to know a little bit of all of them. Having that one cultural reference to connect over with others helped me start a lot of small talk that eventually led to amazing job opportunities and friendships.

As discussed in later chapters, speaking different languages and understanding various cultures can directly lead to job opportunities. You might choose to use your skills to become a cross-cultural trainer, an interpreter, or perhaps a diplomat.

But even if you don't want to work directly in international relations or translations, your knowledge of different languages and cultures opens doors to an array of job opportunities in all industries that others might not have the skills to apply to. For example, applying for an internship program in a completely foreign country is much easier for us (as we are used to living abroad). Many jobs also favor bilingual or trilingual speakers who can better understand different markets around the world.

My biggest advice is to continue honing this advantage you have as a TCT. Humans are forgetful creatures. Even if you had spent more than half of your life speaking a certain language, after merely months of not speaking the language, you can easily forget it completely. We have a head start on language and culture learning. Don't waste this chance assuming you'd be able to remember your languages forever. Continue taking classes in high school, college, and beyond, so you have enough proficiency to proudly write on your resume that you are an expert in that language.

If you are still in a "foreign" country you are not yet accustomed to, take full advantage of it and immerse yourself in the local culture. Go out there and speak the language with local people, watch local television, and listen to local music. While it might be difficult for you now, you'll thank yourself in the future once you have your encyclopedia full of numerous cultures and languages in your brain!

## 2. BEING EMPATHETIC AND OPEN-MINDED

A strength that we, as Third Culture Kids, have been gifted with is a stronger openness and tolerance of diversity than our national counterparts back home.

Scholarly research, in fact, backs this statement. Dewaele and van Oudenhoven's 2009 research found that TCKs have significantly higher scores in the "open-mindedness" dimension of the Multicultural Personality Questionnaire (MPQ) than non-TCKs do.[60] Straffon's 2003 research found that only 3 percent of TCKs attending international schools in Southeast Asia have ethnocentric worldviews, based on the results from

---

60   Jean-Marc Dewaele and Jan Pieter van Oudenhoven, "The effect of multilingualism/multiculturalism on personality: no gain without pain for Third Culture Kids?" *International Journal of Multilingualism* 6, no. 4 (2009): 443-459.

their Intercultural Development Inventory (IDI).[61] Melles and Schwartz's 2012 study also demonstrates that level of exposure to other cultures predicts levels of self-reported prejudicial attitudes, based on 197 TCK participants' scores on the "affective" subscale of the Quick Discrimination Index (QDI).[62]

There may be many reasons behind TCKs' increased tolerance for diversity. One reason may be that their time abroad led to a decrease in xenophobia. Another may be that it developed as a necessity of living in an international community.

This, however, is not to say that every TCK is more open toward diversity. According to Melles and Schwartz, "a few TCKs become more prejudiced as a result of . . . their position of privilege in the host culture."[63]

Many studies, regardless, prove that TCKs are generally more tolerant and unbiased than their monocultural counterparts. You might sense this in your daily lives as a TCK through the many conflicts you have had with your friends and family members back home who might have more conservative worldviews than you do.

---

61   David A Straffon, "Assessing the intercultural sensitivity of high school students attending an international school," International Journal of Intercultural Relations 27, no. 4 (2003): 487-501.

62   Elizabeth A. Melles and Jonathan Schwartz, "Does the third culture kid experience predict level of prejudice?" International Journal of Intercultural Relations 37, no. 2 (2013): 260-267.

63   Ibid.

This comes with a lot of advantages. Grace, for instance, discussed how cultural sensitivity helped her become a better teacher.

"I think I have the cultural sensitivity to the different subtleties of what it means to be an Asian and the expectation that the parents have. Even though my parents didn't have the same expectation for me, I think I understand or am more aware of what parents want from their child. So, when I meet with them for parent-teacher conferences, I know which aspects I can delve into and what the parents would like to hear."

Being more open to diversity and different cultures also come with more opportunities to various experiences. Fareeha believes she interacted with various groups of people and even cuisines that other students might have missed out on during her time at NYU thanks to her openness toward other cultures.

"I think sometimes even as an NYU student you get stuck in this bubble of Washington Square Park or of downtown Manhattan. I think being an international student and a Third Culture Kid, [I could recognize] how many different communities and stories are out there that others might not interact with or recognize immediately. I also think it's just made me really excited to learn about what other people are like and seek different experiences—I'll never say no to trying new types of food."

Others use their interests in equality and tolerance for a greater cause, taking a step to change the world they live in.

Jessica Kim, for instance, is a board member for the USC Asian Pacific American Student Assembly despite the fact that she is not American. She has witnessed the need for Asian empowerment in the United States and empathizes with the Asian-American community—despite never having been a part of it.

Our tolerance also allows us to make a variety of friends. We are good listeners because we are good observers.[64] We are used to observing the "locals" around us and attempting to adapt to our environment. Naturally, instead of pushing our opinion on other people or insisting on our way of life, we listen, observe, and try to understand other people's perspectives. We can also better handle misunderstandings as we have constantly run into such miscommunication all our lives.[65] This makes us great friend material for all kinds of people—and great friends are one of the greatest assets of life.

Despite the advantages, a more open and tolerant attitude always comes with the burden of family members and friends' lack of understanding, and sometimes, even dismissal for our worldview.

This is especially true in a world that is growing more and more nationalistic, exemplified by UK's Brexit decision or Japan's decision to remilitarize. Tolerance is easily seen as an

---

64   Erik Vyhmeister, "Building Identity as a Third Culture Kid | Erik Vyhmeister | TEDxAndrewsUniversity," TEDx Talks, May 26, 2015. Video, 8:06.

65   Ibid.

ineffectual attitude or a failure to choose sides in an increasingly dividing world. This is, perhaps, a reason why a lot of ATCKs choose to move abroad where their differences are more tolerated.

I still do not have the answer for how to cope with conflicts that arise due to a TCK's uniquely tolerant worldview. I have experienced instances in which I wished I wasn't as vocal about my stance on certain issues. I have also experienced instances in which I wish I was more vocal about the issues I care about. I also struggle with questions of whether I've turned too "Western" or if the views I impose upon my "Eastern" friends are a racism of some sort as well.

But I am certain about two things:

First of all, others out there share the same worldview as you, even if they aren't necessarily TCKs.

Second of all, the advantages of an open, tolerant worldview far surpass the disadvantages. You are more likely to learn from those who are different from you and grow into a more globally capable, talented human being than other people who do not have to worry about these issues. Your ability to empathize and care for others will take you further places than you can ever imagine.

I will end on a note from Dae Young Lee, a cross-cultural coach in Korea, on TCKs.

"People can say you are stuck between cultures. In the 21st century, that is actually the best spot to be. Hence, you should define and interpret your position on your own with your own words, not somebody else's words. That's none of their business. Please do not let them say whatever they want to you.

"Telling them that, that's actually an act of kindness to them."

### 3. FLEXIBILITY

"Flexibility has become a modern-day value that everyone wants. But flexibility comes with a cost."

Above is a quote from Maynard Webb, an American businessman.

In our rapidly changing world, flexibility is key to success. Luckily for us TCTs, flexibility is practically our middle name. Having been thrown off into all kinds of different environments in different cultures in different countries, we are quite adept at adjusting to various situations and sometimes creating something new out of them.

The very word "third culture" defines who we are—we are not bound by the established first or second culture. We adapt and we create because we are flexible.

Here's Amy's story from her years at the University of Virginia (UVA).

"[Being a TCK] definitely made me adaptable . . . that could be a strength and sometimes a weakness. It also made me empathetic—also definitely a strength but also a weakness. It's all about how you use it right?"

"I saw myself as the bridge between different cultures—Chinese and American culture. This bridge mentality also connected to almost everything I did."

"For example, I created my own interdisciplinary major. I didn't want to be limited to one thing, so I took a class in every single school at UVA."

Amy's years of living as a TCT provided her with the opportunity to be flexible in her academic endeavors. She did not limit herself to the majors provided by her university. Instead, she created a whole new major for herself and proficiently managed between different classes in different schools.

Just as in Amy's case, you, as a TCT, will be more comfortable with bending the situation provided to better suit your current circumstances.

In order to maximize this potential as a TCT, the first thing you need to do is to embrace your identity as a TCT.

Being swayed by the expectations of other people is easy to do. Do not fall for that trap! You are unique and special *because* you think differently—more flexibly—than those who are only limited to seeing one perspective or culture.

Other people might not understand you at first, and that is normal. The next step is what matters the most. Be persistent with your opinion and viewpoint. Embrace the middle-zone. They are looking for *your* innovative idea.

With the ability of flexibility, you can work in different places instead of being limited to a single location. Many jobs—or even summer internships—require you to relocate to a different city or even a different country. Although other people might be afraid to take that bold step forward, you have the advantage of being able to be wherever you need to be. You are unafraid of changes, and you are used to adapting. In fact, moving to a different place has now become second nature for you, and perhaps you are already fidgeting in your seat, ready to be placed somewhere else.

This also comes with the need to be proactive. When someone offers or mentions a new idea or a new opportunity, be the first one to say that you're up for it! Explain your background of growing up in different countries. Convince them of your flexibility in relocating. This will open up many more opportunities that others might be too afraid to take.

Although the TCT experience haunts us with struggles and insecurities, it also comes with perks that monocultural kids might not enjoy. However, as Amy also mentioned, an advantage can turn into a disadvantage and vice versa. Embrace your traits and identity as a TCT and be proactive in making sure they remain an advantage for you.

Be confident in yourself and in your advantages as a TCT.

You are the global prototype they are all looking for.

## THREE POINT SUMMARY

- Knowing a variety of languages and cultures helps you network with people from different backgrounds.
- Being empathetic and open-minded allows you to appear more amiable to a diverse group of people.
- You also have the advantage of being more flexible than others in terms of creative ideas and in relocations. Use it!

# CHAPTER 11:

# AN INTERVIEW WITH ISABELLE MIN

———

*"Reclaim the power that you regarded as your loss from being uprooted so often. You will discover that there is a reason why you had to go through all the challenges of your life."*

— ISABELLE MIN

Isabelle Min is a professional cultural interpreter, and the founder of the Transition Catalyst Korea Institute (TCK Institute), supporting individual and organizational transformations of those who work in between cultures as a professional coach, facilitator, and conflict mediator. She spent nine years as an adjunct professor at Sungkyunkwan University in Seoul, Korea, and represents the Korea Affiliate for Families in Global Transition.

I was introduced to Isabelle by Kawtar via email. As I have repeatedly emphasized, the TCK community is unbelievably supportive—I had the privilege to talk to all these amazing people just via online interactions.

Isabelle had a calm yet assertive aura to her voice. Though we shared a casual conversation in a casual setting—I was in my dorm and Isabelle in her office—it almost felt like I was sitting at a lecture hall or a TED talk listening to her gracefully tell her story of both strength and vulnerability.

Isabelle is the ultimate TCK, and from my limited knowledge, one of the earlier generations of TCKs in Korea.

Isabelle was born in Washington, DC, as her father was a Korean diplomat stationed in the US at the time. When she was just a few months old, her family moved back to Korea, then to Thailand, and then back to Korea over the course of eight years.

After finishing second grade, Isabelle's family moved again, this time to Italy. She attended a public school in Italy before relocating to Brazil where her first memory of struggle as a TCK begins.

"I was one of their five children, so my parents could not afford to send us all to international schools. By the time we arrived in Brazil, however, they were able to make a huge investment by enrolling me in an American school in Brazil."

"Going to an American school and not speaking a word [of English] was so difficult. Prior to the move, I had begun learning English at the Italian public school—as a foreign language."

Her unfamiliarity with the English language led to immense struggle for teenage Isabelle.

"I was in sixth grade, and in the Italian public school system, it is part of middle school. However, at the American school, I was put in the fifth grade because I couldn't speak English. In a classroom with younger kids, I felt as though I had become deaf and mute, coming from a poor country no one knew about."

A couple years later, once she learned English, Isabelle skipped a grade and was promoted to the ninth grade. But after she overcame one challenge, there came another one: her feat had led to others' misperceiving her as a high-achieving student.

"I was simply catching up with my age group, but I was suddenly considered a 'nerdy Asian' kid. Being at an American school, I had fast absorbed this notion of wanting to be the popular kid, someone who is constantly invited to weekend parties, so it was awful to be labelled as a nerd, especially because that's not how I saw myself."

This desire to become popular, to be recognized, to be seen again—the usual TCT problem—manifested when the family was relocated to Libya, where she was enrolled into a British high school.

Wanting, for once, to become the "popular kid" in her new school, Isabelle hung out with the "cool kids" at school, loosening on her studies. This was in addition to the fact that her entire curriculum had changed from American to English, and her English, while fluent, was American English, which teachers overtly reprimanded. She ended up being sent out to stand in hallways, along with other so called "cool kids." Isabelle recalls that by the end of the semester, at the end of the year party, she had boys lining up to dance with her. After the party, Isabelle remembered feeling disoriented.

"I had set out to become popular and I had made it. But then I realized I was no longer at an American school. My futile attempt to compensate for something that happened else-where struck me as ridiculous."

After her realization in Libya, teenage Isabelle resolved to making her own decisions for herself instead of being consumed with what other people think. One of the first steps toward it involved moving to Milan on her own to live with her older sister, who was studying to become an opera singer. At the small international school, she built lasting friendships with a handful of people whom she really connected with.

"I remember feeling rather lonely and out of place in Milan, away from parents for the first time. Having a good group of reliable friends really helped me. One of them is still in touch with me."

Just as she was getting adjusted to her life in Italy, Isabelle's parents suggested she return to Korea to complete high school in her home country and prepare for the university entrance exam. Repatriating to what she had always believed to be her home country, she was met with yet another culture shock.

"I was worried but didn't anticipate repatriation would be a challenge because I spoke Korean flawlessly. Having gone through so many moves and experiences in recent years, I was gung ho, thinking, 'How difficult could this be?'"

Even though she could read, speak, and write Korean, it took Isabelle at least six months to really comprehend and absorb what was being taught. She was quick to make friends whom she keeps to this day, but she felt misunderstood and misfit to Korean culture.

Moving on to college, she felt she had completely adjusted to her life in Korea, but she was faced with yet another dilemma regarding her identity as a Korean TCT.

"One of the things I remember from those early years of repatriation is how I tried hard not to mix English words when speaking in Korean. I didn't want to stick out by having people notice my fluency in English. Just another of the many ways I tried to fit in."

As she struggled to blend in, she was irritated by the way others, such as Korean-American kids visiting Korea for summer camps, acted as though they had no problem being accepted in the US. Having spent years abroad feeling like an outsider, often cast aside from the main group, Isabelle felt they were disguising the truth of their realities, showing off their English fluency in front of an audience of envious Koreans.

"They stood out to me like a sore thumb, probably because I was dealing with the same internal dilemma. Growing up abroad I had often felt inferior because I couldn't speak their languages and because I didn't know of their ways. Then I repatriated to Korea where I suddenly found myself a token of envy because I spoke English and had lived abroad. This made me wonder whether Korea was any less than those other countries where people spoke English. I could not accept that because as a diplomat's daughter, I was raised to be proud of my country."

She wanted to explain to people that this idea of cultural and linguistic superiority and inferiority is just an illusion, a facade—that speaking five languages does not make you any better or worse than others who are monolingual.

"I remember toying with this internal conflict, which is how I ended up doing intercultural communication and conflict related work today."

Despite the pain of learning each one, speaking five languages has opened multiple opportunities for Isabelle throughout her career as an interpreter and English broadcaster for television and radio. She summed up her relationship with English and her memories abroad as that of "love and pain."

Settled in Korea with a family and a job for decades, Isabelle says she didn't think that she had a choice to live outside Korea.

"As a teenage Third Culture Kid, you don't have a say [in where to go next]. You depend on someone else—your parents, the sponsoring organization—to tell you where to go. So, once

I repatriated, I didn't think I had a choice or a reason to go live anywhere else."

She wonders if she could have made a different decision if she had found another TCK mentor who understood her challenges and insecurities. The impact of multiple moves during her late teens through different school systems (American, British, International, and Korean) had eroded any confidence she may have had to excel in learning.

Today, her memories of repeated transitions and longing for support help her in mentoring young adult TCKs. Since 2010, she has been providing guidance and mentoring meetings for TCKs and parents on and offline through TCK Network as well as through the Korea Affiliate for Families in Global Transition.

Her final word of advice for TCTs speaks to the same ability to transform their painful memories of helplessness into empowerment.

"My advice is that there is a reason why this happened to you. You're in that unique place to learn about how it feels to be where you are, and you are in that unique place to do something about it.

"So, reclaim your power. Reclaim your power to challenge life regardless of anything else. Reclaim the power that you regarded as your loss from being uprooted so often. Reclaim your power, and you will discover that there is a reason why you had to go through all the challenges and all the difficulties of your life."

"This is important because we are the prototype of a global citizen. Despite all the inequality and separation in the world, we are already here—the global people."

"We are the global prototype."

"It's one thing to know about diversity and it's another to live it, and we are the people who live it."

How can you reclaim your power as the global prototype today?

# CHAPTER 12:

# WHAT'S AHEAD?
# STORIES FROM ATCKS

―――

*"One day, he said he wanted to be president,*
*but he didn't say what country."*[66]

— BARRACK OBAMA'S PRIMARY SCHOOL TEACHER

The previous chapters have discussed the Third Culture *Teen* experience—of being in between a Third Culture Kid and an Adult Third Culture Kid. The fortunate (or perhaps unfortunate depending on how you view it) part of being a TCT is that it is not going to last forever.

Personally, I grew out of being a "teen" just two years ago. The transition came very abruptly. Most of the time, I feel out of sync with my actual age. I would not dare to call myself

―――

66  *Inside Edition.* "Inside the Home Where Obama Grew Up in Indonesia." August 13, 2019. Video, 1:47.

an "adult" quite yet. Inside, I still feel like I'm still the same fifteen-year-old girl who listened to punk music.

Yet, I now experience little moments in which the fact that I'm an adult begins to sink in. It's when I don't find it too terrifying to talk to other adults—deliverymen or customer service—on the phone. It's when I cook food on my own without looking up a recipe on YouTube. It's when I realize I don't really feel the same urge to look "cool" on Instagram.

Because I'm still taking little baby steps toward adulthood, I have handed this chapter over to more *grown-up* adults instead.

In this chapter, you will get an overview of what's ahead in life for TCTs. You will hear from ATCKs of various backgrounds—some who are famous celebrities and others whom you may find more familiar—and how their multicultural backgrounds influenced the adult they have become today.

## THE ATCK: AN OVERVIEW

Morgan Byttner, from the University of Arkansas, conducted an extensive survey of over two hundred ATCKs aged 18 to 64.

According to the survey, the most popular major amongst ATCKs is international studies and its related fields, accounting for more than 18 percent of the ATCKs surveyed. Social sciences came in second with 14 percent.[67]

---

67  Morgan Byttner, "Career Choices and the Influence of Third Culture Kids on International Relations" (undergraduate honors thesis, University of Arkansas, Fayetteville, 2012), 24.

Almost half of all respondents also listed a second major, a quarter of which were international relations-related fields. Another popular second major was foreign language, accounting for 11 percent of all second majors listed.[68]

Not surprisingly, nearly 66 percent of participants agreed that their experiences as a TCK shaped their academic interests and career choice. Growing up as TCKs and later as TCTs, ATCKs continue to be interested in connecting bridges between different cultures and different languages—just as they have been doing their whole lives.[69]

I especially find it interesting that many of them chose to have a second major related to international relations or foreign languages. Even ATCKs who did not choose to pursue a career in international relations reported that they wanted to dive deeper into this topic in college.

Regarding their career choices, a majority of ATCKs chose not to work for the government.

Instead, many of them chose careers that involved cross-cultural understanding or foreign languages.[70]

Almost 80 percent of respondents answered that they either already work in or want to work in a job that requires exten-

---

68  Ibid.

69  Ibid., 26.

70  Ibid.

sive travel, and over 50 percent of them answered that they wanted to "move back overseas."[71]

It has also been discovered in earlier studies by scholars Ruth Hill Useem and Ann Baker Cottrell that TCKs are four times more likely to earn a bachelor's degree, and 80 percent of them become professionals, executives, or managers.[72] Because the study is somewhat outdated, its accuracy in today's world is unclear. Yet, it does suggest that ATCKs are more likely to rise to high positions in their career than to not.

The international lifestyle continues to influence ATCKs— even after they have moved out of their parents' household. This influence often extends to majors in college and lifelong careers.

The perfect instance of continued interest in international relations can be found in Kawtar, a cross-cultural trainer.

## KAWTAR EL ALAOUI: CROSS-CULTURAL TRAINER

Kawtar is the founder & CEO of Conscious Togetherness, Inc., where she designs and facilitates leadership, conflict resolution, and cross-cultural communication workshops. You can find her story and her services on her website: www.kawtarelalaoui.ca.

---

71   Ibid., 31.

72   Ann Baker Cottrell and Ruth Hill Useem, "TCKs Four Times More Likely to Earn Bachelor's Degrees," *TCK World: The Official Home of Third Culture Kids,* April 11, 2009.

Running out of people in my social circle to interview and hear stories from, I randomly googled "TCK groups" and found a massive Facebook group where TCKs connect with each other. When I was accepted as a member, I uploaded a post about interview opportunities with low expectations for getting responses from anyone. To my surprise, many people were only happy to help out—and Kawtar was the first person to offer her help.

Being the TCKs we are, our first questions were time zones, and we finally worked out a time for a Zoom conversation together.

Even from the computer screen, I could feel Kawtar's aura as a speaker and a CEO. She had a confident smile as she told me her journey as a TCK and an ATCK using her multicultural background to make this world a better place.

Kawtar was born in Morocco to Moroccan parents. When her parents separated and her mother remarried a Canadian man, she had to go back and forth between Canada and Morocco at the age of ten. She remembers always having to manage between two homes and two cultures—spending some of her summer and her school year in Canada and the rest of her school years in Morocco. She struggled to find acceptance in either culture.

She specifically recalled the time she was a teenager in Morocco with her family. When her father saw her with makeup on, he told her that she could not leave the house with makeup like that.

"I was just so confused because I had just come back from Canada where girls wear makeup all the time. I didn't get it: Why is it that it's so casual and normal there, and here, it's so frowned upon? It's one moment that really symbolizes a lot of the clashes that I lived with between the cultures."

Kawtar is representative of the generation of ATCKs who only learned about the term "TCK" after becoming an adult. Before learning that she was a Third Culture Kid, Kawtar always felt alone and out of place.

"When I grew up and I became an adult, I was trying to find my identity. I was trying to sift through all of that baggage."

"At first, not consciously. I was just trying to find my way [and] find where I belong. My values were always clashing. I would be living in Canada but acting very Moroccan. Yet, when I'm with Moroccans I would never be Moroccan enough, always going into the in-between space. . . I found myself alone in it for the most part."

Once she sifted through her emotional baggage and came to terms with the fact that she was a Third Culture Kid, she found opening up to people from other cultures was much easier.

At that point, she grew a strong desire to use her experience of being in the "in-between space" to help others. She received instruction to become a cross-cultural trainer and eventually founded her own global leadership entity to serve the creation of a more empathetic and connected world. Weaving together her professional skills with her personal experiences, she designed connecting and empowering programs at the intersection of personal development, leadership training, communication and conflict transformation, cultural understanding, and diversity and inclusion.

She has also spent the last seven years of her life as a global nomad and an ATCK mother raising a TCK child, living in South Korea for four years and currently residing in Mumbai, India.

"Culture has become such an important part of my identity that it's also part of what I do for work—from a cross-cultural trainer to a coach. For me, what it really taught me is that beyond those layers where we're different, we're actually all the same."

"And that's what really connects to my work and my message."

## BARACK OBAMA: FORTY-FOURTH PRESIDENT OF THE UNITED STATES

While Byttner's survey suggests that most ATCKs choose not to work for the government, some certainly do. In fact, former President of the United States Barack Obama is an ATCK as well.

Barrack Obama, as many people know, is an American attorney and politician who served as the forty-fourth President of the United States from 2009 to 2017. What a lot of people might not know is that he is also a Third Culture Kid.

Obama was born in Hawaii to a Kenyan father and an American mother. From birth, he was, hence, a Cross-Cultural Kid, but after his mother married an Indonesian grad student in Hawaii and the whole family moved to central Jakarta in 1967, Obama officially became a Third Culture Kid.[73]

When he first arrived in Indonesia, Obama did not speak a single line of Indonesian.

Yet the family tried their best to live just as the locals did. The first house that the family moved to was in a middle-class neighborhood in Jakarta. A modest two-story home without a fridge but a large backyard teeming with animals, the house was more or less like many of the other middle-class houses near it.[74]

Obama's Indonesian childhood friends recall that Obama—back then referred to as 'Barry'—was the first Black kid the neighborhood had seen.

"Barry had to endure endless teasing about his curly black hair," Barry's friend recalled in an interview.[75]

Despite his evident physical and cultural differences from everyone around him, Obama's parents raised him much like the other Indonesian children and encouraged him to embrace the local Jakarta culture.

---

73 *Inside Edition.* "Inside the Home Where Obama Grew Up in Indonesia." August 13, 2019. Video, 1:15.

74 Ibid., 2:26

75 Ibid., 2:15

Obama's memoir, *Dreams from My Father*, encapsulates the adventure of Obama's life as a TCK:

*It had taken me less than six months to learn Indonesia's language, its customs, and its legends. I had survived chicken pox, measles, and the sting of my teachers' bamboo switches. . . With Lolo [Obama's stepfather], I learned how to eat small green chili peppers raw with dinner (plenty of rice), and, away from the dinner table, I was introduced to dog meat (tough), snake meat (tougher), and roasted grasshopper (crunchy). That's how things were, one long adventure, the bounty of a young boy's life.[76]*

When the time came for school, Obama first attended a private Catholic grammar school and later a neighborhood public school.

Obama was treated just like another Indonesian child—because he was registered as one. In his records "Barry Soetoro's" nationality was recorded simply as "Indonesian."[77]

Yet, he always stood out among his Indonesian friends—not only because of his tall height and his curly hair but because of his large dreams.

---

76   Barack Obama, *Dreams From My Father* (New York: Three Rivers Press, 2004), 156.

77   *Inside Edition.* "Inside the Home Where Obama Grew Up in Indonesia." August 13, 2019. Video, 2:57.

"One day, he said he wanted to be president, but he didn't say what country," Obama's primary school teacher told the interviewers at Inside Edition in 2008.[78]

At school, Obama became completely fluent in Indonesian and was especially skilled in mathematics.

A more formative time in Obama's life in Indonesia was in his public school. The school reflected the local population in that it was 90 percent Muslim. Yet, it also respected diversity among its students by not only offering Muslim worship time but also a separate Christian chapel time for Christian students.[79]

In 1971, Obama left the family home and returned to his home country. Yet he continued to be treated as an "outsider." A fatherless boy who had just moved from Indonesia, he did not share much in common with the neighborhood boys.

Flash forward to 2008, Obama was dragged down by other candidates and the press for being different from other Americans. Obama was accused of being raised in a radical Muslim school and was also "accused" of being Muslim himself. Rumors surfaced about Obama's not being American, and he was even pushed to provide a birth certificate.[80]

---

78 Ibid., 1:47.

79 Margie Mason, "Obama pushes tolerance, respect in childhood home, Jakarta," *Washington Post*, July 2, 2017.

80 Ibid.

Despite such challenges, Obama was elected as America's forty-fourth president and tried his best to unite his divided country during his time in the office.

In 2010, when he returned to Jakarta, this time not just as a foreigner child, but as the President of the United States, he expressed how important his time in Indonesia had been for him as a leader and a human being.

"My time here made me cherish respect for people's differences."[81]

To the roaring Indonesian crowd, he yelled in fluent Indonesian,

"Indonesia bagian dari diri saya!" or "Indonesia is part of me!"[82]

During the time of Obama's presidency, public opinion of the US [in Indonesia] improved dramatically, and Obama, in this way, acted as the connecting bridge between his childhood home and his home country.

Although Obama had a difficult time adjusting to Indonesia as a foreigner and was taken down by the American public for his time abroad, he used these experiences to his advantage, leading America as an understanding and accepting president.

---

81   Ibid.

82   Ibid.

## LINDIE BOTES: UI/UX DESIGNER & POLYGLOT YOUTUBER

Lindie Botes is a designer and language YouTuber based in Singapore. Lindie, while born in South Africa, spent the majority of her life outside of her passport country. Parts of her childhood and middle school years were spent in France, Pakistan, and the UAE. During her university years in South Africa, the rest of her family moved to Japan, leading Lindie to briefly move to Japan for an internship as well. After working briefly in South Africa, she has recently moved to Singapore for a new job.

I first got to know Lindie's YouTube channel through her hilarious five-million-view-video that went viral in Korea. It was a video of her speaking Korean fluently after anesthesia. But what got me subscribed to her channel was her emotional video on the experience of being a Third Culture Kid.

In her video, Lindie specifically recalls her return to South Africa in ninth grade. She had no friends, and she had no idea what some of the subjects they were learning at school were.

"I'm really blessed to have my childhood . . . but it was hard . . . When somebody tells me they've been friends with someone for twelve years, I'm like, 'What? How is this real?'"[83]

But moreover, she found it extremely hard to form a solid relationship with her friends at school. She struggled with

---

83  *Lindie Botes,* "Joys and challenges of being a Third Culture Kid | Where is home?" April 16, 2018. Video, 1:43.

finding things that connected her to her South African classmates who grew up with the same culture all their lives—listening to the same music and enjoying the same sports—none of which she knew about.

"In high school, I was so concerned with fitting in. It was an all-girls school too, and I really felt like an outsider: the South African with an American accent. I tried so hard to adopt a South African accent . . . working so hard to be like my peers."

But despite her efforts, she never felt comfortable or safe in South Africa.

"I just feel more energized and thriving if I'm in a different country. It feels very stagnant in South Africa."

Instead of attempting to find an answer within her local environment, she expanded her interests *even* further out into the world. She got immersed in French and art, and then K-pop, which led her to a relevant Vietnamese video, which led her to the Vietnamese language.

She fell in love with language learning because she felt that learning languages created a safe space of her own.

"Being made up of different cultures, I think that languages are a safe space for me to feel comfortable in. Overall, speaking different languages helps me form this unique identity that is Lindie, which is not tied to my passport country or where I grew up."

Even after multiple rejections, she continued to reach out to job opportunities in countries like Japan and Korea, which she grew an interest in during her language-learning journey.

After briefly working in South Africa, she made the brave decision to move to Singapore—a whole new country she had never lived in before. She now also has a very active YouTube channel of over one hundred thousand subscribers and was invited to speak at an international polyglot conference in Japan.

Reflecting back on her teenage years, Lindie tells her teenage self the following words:

"Don't worry about what people think of you and force yourself to try and fit in, but be more comfortable with what your background is, who you are, and know that things will turn out okay. . ."

"What makes me *me* is my background and the languages I speak and the people who appreciate me for I am. I don't need to change myself to fit into them."

## FREDDIE MERCURY (FARROKH BULSARA): MUSICIAN

While the above figures have used their TCK background to their advantage, some ATCKs completely disregarded their TCK background.

One of these ATCKs is Farrokh Bulsara, better known as Freddie Mercury, the legendary vocalist of the British band Queen.

Mercury's original name is Farrokh Bulsara, and he was born in Zanzibar, Tanzania, to Indian Parsi parents on September 5, 1946.[84] A large portion of Mercury's childhood was spent in India, where he learned to play piano at the age of seven.

Mercury faced alienation and his first internal conflict about his identity when he was sent to a boarding school in Bombay, India. He was made fun of as Buckie because of his buckteeth and also because of his skin color.[85]

Mercury faced an even greater identity crisis when he moved to England at the age of seventeen. There, Mercury was teased for his Indian accent.[86]

Mercury chose to blend into—and then later stand out in—the dismissive British community around him, completely abandoning his identity and creating a new one.

In 1971, he formed the band Queen and gave himself the new name that we know today: Freddie Mercury. Mercury's talent and flamboyancy were embraced by the world, and Mercury was invincible. By taking on a completely different persona, he completely eradicated any sign of "foreignness" within him.

In his article on Mercury, WonSeop Suh writes,

---

84 "Freddie Mercury's Complex Relationship with Zanzibar," *BBC,* October 23, 2018.

85 Ibid.

86 WonSeop Suh, "Surprise TCK: Freddie Mercury," *Cultures: The Global Multicultural Magazine,* May 1, 2014.

"Although his stage name conceals his TCK origin, I always like to believe that the revolutionary sounds and looks he has created an artist come from the cultural diversity that lives within him."[87]

Did Mercury live a happy life by completely abandoning his past and concealing his cultural identity?

I guess we'll never know.

### AMY MCMILLEN: AUTHOR & FORMER PRODUCT MANAGER

We often like to believe that some kind of answer lies beyond a certain place, time, or age.

I remember coming to college with big expectations about all the wisdom and self-discovery that would come with semi-adulthood, only to find out that while I did make new friends and learned new lessons, I could never find solid answers to questions about who I really am.

My conversation with Amy, a fellow author with the same publisher, reminded me that the journey to working out your identity—especially as a Third Culture Kid—is one that will forever be ongoing.

Amy is a former product manager from New York who is now on a creative sabbatical. Before New York, she went to school in Virginia, where she had lived since she was ten. She

---

87  Ibid.

spent her childhood years in China, where she was born. She is half Chinese and half American and has grown up always feeling othered from her environment.

"I think part of being a Third Culture Kid is feeling like you don't belong anywhere, and I've definitely felt othered in many ways—regardless of whether I'm in China or in the US."

Being half white, she has always felt like a foreigner in the country she was born in. While she has beautiful childhood memories from China, she also cherished her summers in the US. When her family actually moved to the US when she got older, however, her American life was nothing like the summers she spent there.

"It would be like Disneyland or just seeing family. Sunshine and rainbow and all that. And then, we actually moved to Virginia. It was very much not that."

In her small private Christian school in Virginia, she was one of the two Asian kids at her school, the other being her Filipino friend.

"I felt like I was othered. . .I just didn't really feel like I belonged as an American."

Amy overcame the feeling of being the "other" at school when she simply accepted her identity for who she was.

"I think I just accepted it. It wasn't really something I had to conquer, and ultimately I kind of knew that it was my place."

When she accepted the innate uncertainty that comes with her identity, she realized that her experiences as a Third Culture Kid could actually be used to her advantage.

"I saw myself as the bridge between different cultures—Chinese and American culture through my parents. This bridge mentality also connected to almost everything I did."

"I would say those experiences directly came from living in very different types of environments from a young age. And the adaptability I believe that comes from being a TCK showed me that I can understand others."

That did not, however, mean that she had all the answers to her questions in life. Like many other college kids, she had a difficult time trying to find her place in the world. Although she eventually found a great job in New York and small places in New York grew on her enough for her to call it "home," she quit her job to take a sabbatical and reflect back on her life and future plans.

"I always felt like there was a task I was following, and at times, I questioned whether these choices are right for me. Of course, I decided to do all those things myself, but you never know until you take a step back and take time to contemplate what you actually like to do and what you do."

During her sabbatical, she also decided to trace back her cultural roots and visited China for six weeks. She had not been back to China for thirteen years since she left.

She made sure to go to major tourist spots, but more importantly, she visited her old neighborhood and even her old apartment. While China has changed so much due to technological advancements, she realized, to her surprise, that a lot remained the same.

"It was interesting the way it kind of felt the same way. It was just like when I was with my family and eating hot pot. It felt almost the same exact way."

When asked if she found any new answers about her cultural identity in China, she gave me a surprising answer.

"I would say I got to question my identity more while I was there. The second I got off the airplane I was already being stared at constantly in Chengdu[, China]. That was interesting to me because I didn't think I looked too foreign, but I guess I do."

"And that led to a whole other series of questions, like, 'Do I feel more Chinese, or do I feel more American?' 'What does being American feel like?' I don't know. I don't know if I ever got any answers to these questions."

Amy's journey to finding the answers to her identity as a biracial Third Culture Kid is still an ongoing process—just as it is for all of us.

We might find the answers in ten, twenty, or thirty years, or perhaps never really.

But just as Amy's sabbatical led her to China and to the publication of a new book on emotional intelligence, we will also never know what exciting places this journey might take us.

* * *

You have heard stories from five different ATCKs. You can find more ATCK stories from the earlier mini chapters on Grace Lee and Isabelle Min.

While some of them are successful celebrities, others are still going through their journey of discovering where they want to be in the world. While some of them fully embraced their ATCK identity and used it to their advantage, others have completely disregarded their cultural identity.

Regardless of where we will be and whatever path of life we choose, one thing is clear: a spark that glows within ATCKs. ATCKs, having been exposed to a variety of cultures and lifestyles, have experiences that others have taken their whole lives to have.

Where will you be in ten years?

What kind of an ATCK would you want to be for the next generation of TCTs?

# CHAPTER 13:

# YOUR STORY

———

*"It's always what the military needs, what the foreign service needs, what the missionaries need. So, I guess that makes a lot of artists, because you want to express yourself."*[88]

— DONNA MUSIL

Even today, many of the popular posts in the TCK subreddit are titled "Am I a TCK?" or "Do I count as a TCK?" The term TCK remains a fairly obscure and niche term, and many TCKs today do not even recognize that they are TCKs.

A lot of this comes from the fact that there just aren't enough TCK stories told in the world. (Although the "immigrant experience" stories are definitely being told a lot more today, which I also appreciate!) The TCK experience is not

---

88   Shelley Jones, "Does a Nomadic Childhood Lead to a More Creative Life? Uprooted Kids," *Huck Magazine*, July 22 2015.

normalized enough globally to be recognized as a legitimate label of identity and a legitimate community of people with shared experiences.

The only way to improve this situation and to empower TCKs around the world is to tell the TCK story.

One of the many ways you might do this is by writing a book entirely dedicated to TCKs, as Rachel, Ruth, or I have. But whatever career paths or interests you are led to, they can all be tools to tell the TCK story.

In this chapter, I, as a filmmaker, want to give a shout-out to all the TCK storytellers and artists out there.

The arts is a career path that is not as frequently associated with TCKs as much as politics or business are. TCK artists, however, have so many stories to share with the world through their works—some of them filled with happiness, some of them excitement, and a lot of them of loneliness and loss.

## THE FILMMAKERS

In her article, scholar Shelley Jones attributes many TCKs turn to art in adulthood to their need to express their mixed sense of roots.[89]

TCK filmmaker Donna Musil attests to this need for expression. In her interview with Jones, she shared how growing up as a military/army brat TCK (a subset of TCKs who moved

---

89  Ibid.

between countries due to their parents' military career) fueled her desire to tell stories.

"It's always what the military needs, what the foreign service needs, what the missionaries need. So, I guess that makes a lot of artists, because you want to express yourself."[90]

Musil was raised an army brat and has lived in Germany, Korea, Ireland, Denmark, and France, in addition to various cities throughout the United States. Her father was a JAG officer and a military judge. When she was sixteen, her father passed away, and two weeks later, her family moved to Columbus, Georgia, where she finished high school.[91]

For the next twenty years, Donna moved nineteen more times, graduated college, and worked in a variety of jobs, but always felt "different" from her fellow Americans.[92]

In 1997, she learned that she was not alone. While surfing the internet, Donna discovered a website for her high school in Daegu, Korea. A few weeks later, she attended an impromptu reunion in Washington, DC. It was revelatory. For the first time, Donna felt like she "belonged" somewhere. The reunion prompted her to begin her journey "home."[93] Her journey

---

90  Ibid.

91  Brats Without Borders, Inc. "Filmmaker," *Brats: Our Journey Home*, accessed April 1, 2020.

92  Brats Without Borders, Inc. "About the Film," *Brats: Our Journey Home*, accessed April 1, 2020.

93  Ibid.

home was an artistic one—a journey of filmmaking and storytelling to help others like her feel more understood.

In 2006, Musil wrote and directed the award-winning 2006 documentary film *Brats: Our Journey Home,* a film that tells the story of military brats. The film was featured on CNN's *This Week at War* and NPR's *All Things Considered* and has been broadcast on Armed Forces Network Television in 178 countries around the world.[94]

*Brats: Our Journey Home* is an especially interesting work of art in that it not only features *one* ATCK artist but *two.* The film is narrated by and features the music of another military brat ATCK, Kris Kristofferson, a singer-songwriter. It also stars author Mary Edwards Wertsch, author of one of the first books on military brats, *Military Brats: Legacies of Childhood Inside the Fortress.*[95]

Musil has written on the website for the film that Wertsch's book was an important source of inspiration for her film. She has included a quote from the introduction to Wertsch's book on the website.

"I thought I was singular in all this, one of a kind. From Mary's book, I discovered that I speak in the multi-tongued, deep-throated voice of my tribe. . . [I]t's a language I was not even aware I spoke . . . a secret family I did not know I had. . . Military brats, my lost tribe, spent their entire youth

---

94 Ibid.

95 Ibid.

in service to this country, and no one even knew we were there."[96]

After the film's success, Musil founded a nonprofit organization called Brats Without Borders, Inc., to provide educational materials, outreach, and support to military-connected "brats" and other TCKs of all ages.[97]

Brats Without Borders still remains an active nonprofit organization that also manages Facebook communities for military brats—the link to which can be found in the "Additional Resources" section of the book.

Musil's artistic pursuit as a filmmaker, hence, led to a collaborative project between a TCK singer, a TCK author, and other TCKs, that eventually even brought in a nonprofit organization to support even more military brat TCKs around the world. Amazingly, one story led to a collection of multiple stories, and those stories continue to help a community of TCKs today feel more understood and represented.

Many other filmmakers portray the Third Culture Kid experience in their works.

For instance, Rahul Gandotra is the writer/director/producer of one of the most well-known TCK films, *The Road Home* (2010).

---

96   Ibid.

97   Brats Without Borders, Inc. "The Nonprofit," *Brats: Our Journey Home,* accessed April 1, 2020.

Rahul Gandotra is a TCK filmmaker born in Belfast, Northern Ireland, who grew up in eight countries across Europe, the Middle East, Asia, and America. His international childhood has been a major inspiration and influence on his filmmaking career.[98]

He traveled to the Himalayas to direct *The Road Home*. *The Road Home* is Gandotra's autobiographical story, telling the story of a young boy who was sent by his parents to an international boarding school in the Himalayas; yet, struggling to fit into the school there, he attempts to walk back to his home in England.[99] The short film went on to win many awards at film festivals around the world and was finally nominated for the British Independent Film Awards and shortlisted for the Academy Awards.[100]

You can watch the award-winning short film, *The Road Home* for free:

www.roadhomefilm.com/roadhomefilm

Another filmmaker telling the story of TCKs is Ema Ryan Yamazaki. Ema is a documentary filmmaker and editor, raised by a Japanese mother and a British father.[101]

---

98  "Director," Road Home Film, accessed April 1, 2020.

99  "About, " Road Home Film, accessed April 1, 2020.

100 Ibid.

101 "About," Ema Ryan Yamazaki, accessed April 1, 2020.

Her 2012 documentary short *Neither Here nor There* interviews six different Third Culture Kids from different corners of the world.

Below is the description of the film from the film's website:

"When Home is no where. And everywhere."

"*Neither Here Nor There* is a thirty-five-minute documentary that explores cultural identity for people who have grown up in places other than their home culture, known as Third Culture Kids. Through the stories of six subjects, the film investigates the often overlooked effects on adults who had international upbringings, their struggles to fit in and an eternal search to belong."

"The film is also a self-exploratory journey for the filmmaker, a Japanese-British raised bi-culturally and in an international school system, who now lives in New York. In her last year of college, she attempts to figure out what she is in the context of the world."[102]

The film has been screened at various film festivals and educational conferences around the world.

If the film interests you, you can purchase the DVD of the film on the website:

www.neitherherenorthere-thefilm.com/watchit.html

---

102  "Story," Ema Ryan Yamazaki, accessed April 1, 2020.

Many student filmmakers of this upcoming generation have TCK backgrounds. We, for instance, have heard the story of my friend Kayla who studies film and television production at USC's School of Cinematic Arts.

I, myself, am an aspiring filmmaker as well—and I can't wait to tell more TCK stories through this amazing audio-visual medium!

## THE WRITERS

Writing nonfiction—and fiction—books about the TCK experience is another way in which TCKs share their stories with the world.

As I have already introduced writers such as Ruth Van Reken or Rachel Pieh Jones who have published nonfiction/academic works on the TCK experience, in this chapter, I want to shed light on ATCK fiction writers.

Works by TCKs share many common themes related to the TCK experience.

In fact, Antje Rauwerda, associate professor of British and postcolonial literature at Goucher College, uses the term "TCLiterature" to describe the body of work written by TCK authors.[103]

---

103  Antje M. Rauwerda, "Expatriate Versus Third Culture (Chris Pavone Vs. Belinda Bauer)," *Third Culture Literature* (blog), March 21, 2017.

According to Rauwerda, TCLiterature works have five common features:

1. the outcome of—or specifically deal with—a third culture kid context, and comprise
2. international settings
3. losses
4. disenfranchisement
5. guilt[104]

Rauwerda specifically compares expat literature and TCK literature in her blog post. She explains that TCLiterature is different from expat literature in that TCLiterature often features "importance of international mobility and detachment from 'home' *during the developmental years. . .* If you grow up aware you are an outsider, that feeling persists into adulthood (which adds up to TCKness)."[105]

This is different from expat literature in that in the expat experience (traveling abroad as an adult), "you may feel like an outsider when you travel *but you retain the conviction that you do . . . have a home somewhere.*"[106]

Author Nina Bouraoui, for instance, is an exemplary TCLiterature author.

---

104  Ibid.

105  Ibid.

106  Ibid.

Bouraoui was born in France in 1967 to an Algerian father and a French mother and grew up in France, Algeria, Switzerland, and the UAE.[107]

Her works are largely auto-fictional accounts written in the first person and thus frequently center on the experience of living as a young expat in a foreign country.

Childhood is also a recurrent theme in Bouraoui's work, and it is a space that is intimately connected to wildness and sensuality. Childhood, interestingly enough, is closely associated with *territory* in her auto-fictional texts.[108]

Her novel *Le Jour du séisme*, for instance, is her childhood reiteration of the landscape of Algeria. As writer Amaleena Damlé describes, *Le Jour du séisme*

"Starts and jolts with rhythmic uncertainty and territorial instability, as linguistic fragmentation and repetition link the fluctuations of subjectivity to the trembling of the earth ravaged by war and violence."[109]

*Le Jour du séisme* also juxtaposes the protagonist's national identity and gendered identity, embodying the ongoing ATCK struggle of finding one's identity.[110]

---

107  Amaleena Damlé, "Nina Bouraoui," Institute of Modern Language Research, accessed April 1, 2020.

108  Ibid.

109  Ibid.

110  Ibid.

I especially want to quote the following line of another one of Bouraoui's works, *Tomboy*, which perfectly captures the TCK struggle of unbelonging:

"Forever split between this one and that one, enduring a fractured identity, seeing myself as divided."[111]

Even within works by TCK authors that do not directly discuss the TCK experience, you can still find traces of similar themes.

For instance, Belinda Bauer—an ATCK who grew up in England and South Africa—wrote a murder mystery, *Blacklands*, which tells the story of a boy murdered by a pedophile and his younger brother's efforts to find out what happened to the corpse.[112]

As Rauwerda explains, although the book does not explicitly discuss the expat experience, the story still centers around the "extremes of *what a child may lose* and how it wracks them to try and reclaim what has been lost to them."[113]

Such emphasis on loss—specifically, loss during childhood—places Bauer's mystery novel within the TCLiterature genre.

Because works of literature are often tied to a specific era of a specific nation, many TCK authors often write stories that do not belong in a particular geographical region,

---

111  Nina Bouraoui, Tomboy (Lincoln: U of Nebraska Press, 2007), 101.

112  Antje M. Rauwerda, "Expatriate Versus Third Culture (Chris Pavone Vs. Belinda Bauer)," *Third Culture Literature* (blog), March 21, 2017.

113  Ibid.

thereby finding the need to have a genre of their own. We should accept works by TCK authors with their specific term, whether it be "TCLiterature" or "TCK Literature."

TCK authors, as scholar Jessica Sanfilippo-Schulz puts it, "deserve their own lens of literature through which [their] writings can be analyzed."[114]

## THE MUSICIANS
Similar themes are also explored by successful TCK musicians across the globe.

For instance, Sinkane, who grew up in the UK, Sudan, and the United States, is a singer-songwriter. Sinkane's songs are combinations of different genres across the continent, representing the different geographical regions he has grown up in. His songs are usually described as a mixture of "krautrock, proc rock, electronica, free jazz, and funk rock with Sudanese pop."[115]

The lyrics in his songs also portray his childhood experiences of rootlessness, as shown in one of his songs "Runnin'." In "Runnin'," the line "gotta keep on runnin'" is repeated multiple times, embodying the sense of restlessness that comes from living without a grounded home.[116]

---

114 Jessica Sanfilippo-Schulz, "Escaping National Tags and Embracing Diversity: Third Culture Kid Songwriters," *Open Cultural Studies* 2 (2018): 12.

115 "Sinkane," BBC Music, BBC, accessed April 1, 2020.

116 Jessica Sanfilippo-Schulz, "Escaping National Tags and Embracing Diversity: Third Culture Kid Songwriters," *Open Cultural Studies* 2

British folk singer Tanita Tikaram is another TCK musician. Tikaram was born in Germany to a Malaysian mother and an Indo-Fijian British Army officer father (making her another military brat artist). She spent her childhood years in Germany before moving to England.[117]

Many of Tikaram's songs also discuss the theme of failure to belong somewhere.

In her song, "My Enemy," for example, the lyrics go as follows:

"If I could fly to find out where my place is find out where my place is above the skies . . . to leave the sorrow in this world."[118]

Yet, not all works by TCKs solely discuss the darker sides of the TCK experience.

We can turn to, for instance, Haikaa, a Japan-born singer who was raised in the US, Ecuador, and Singapore.

---

(2018): 16.

117  Colin Larkin, *The Virgin Encyclopedia of Popular Music* (London: Virgin Books, 1997), 1001.

118  Tanita Tikaram, "My Enemy," by Matt Radford and Tanita Tikaram, track 10 on *Closer to the People,* Ear Music, compact disc.

In her book, she discusses how the TCK experience was an invaluable asset to her as a singer:

"Needless to say, the sense of belonging wasn't really a part of my life. I was too Eastern for some, too Western for others, too sexy for some, too serious for others, and so on . . . However, as I got older, what was once a source of confusion has become one of my greatest treasures."[119]

One of her most famous songs, "Work of Art," truly highlights the role TCKs can play as a bridge between different countries and cultures.

"Work of Art" is a song about embracing yourself for who you are. The lyrics go as follows:

"Just because you've never seen a combination like me it doesn't have to mean I don't have to be seen."[120]

Haikaa recorded the song in as many languages as she could and went on a "cyber global trip" in search of lyricists who could do versions of her song in different languages.

---

119  Haikaa Yamamoto, *What Is Diversity?: A Work of Art to Celebrate a Diverse World* (Scotts Valley: CreateSpace Independent Pub, 2012), 3.

120  Haikaa, "Work of Art," by Haikaa, Haikaa Music, track 1 on *Work of Art*, 2011, YouTube.

Her final recording of "Work of Art" ended up being an eight-minute song sung in Arabic, Armenian, Bulgarian, Cantonese, Danish, Dutch, English, French, German, Greek, Hebrew, Italian, Japanese, Korean, Mandarin, Portuguese, Spanish, Turkish, and two indigenous languages of Gurarani M'Bya and Lushootseed.[121]

Through her music, Haikaa connected the world with her message of positivity and empathy.

If you aspire to be a TCK artist, look up the numerous TCK artists out there who, by expressing their stories through art, are on a journey of healing not only their audiences who can relate to the stories told, but also themselves.

Think about how the medium you have chosen can be effectively used to tell the TCK story.

But even without necessarily being an artist, you can always be a part of telling the TCK story.

You can start by following the simple steps below:

1. Use the term "TCK" to describe yourself to others. Make the term more known to non-TCKs!
2. Take a part in publishing articles for TCK websites or for multicultural journals. They want to hear your story.

---

121 Jessica Sanfilippo-Schulz, "Escaping National Tags and Embracing Diversity: Third Culture Kid Songwriters," *Open Cultural Studies* 2 (2018): 19.

3. Be conscious of your TCK background in whatever career you go in to and share your story with other people in your industry.
4. Be a mentor to other TCKs who want to go into the same industry as you.

You have now heard my stories, the stories of other TCKs, and even the variety of beautiful mediums of art that these stories have been told through.

Now you must go out into the world and tell *your* TCT story.

What is *your* story? How do you plan on telling it?

---

## THREE POINT SUMMARY

- Many TCK filmmakers and musicians are out there telling the TCK story through their works. Even if their works do not explicitly deal with the TCK experience, they still embody TCK themes of unbelonging or loss.
- The term "TCK Literature" or "TCLiterature" is used to describe literature by TCK writers. Since literature is often grouped according to their geographical region or time in history, TCK authors should have their own term as well.
- Even if you're not an artist or a storyteller, you can still be a part of telling the TCK story by telling your TCK story to those around you.

# PART 5:

# CONCLUSION & ADDITIONAL RESOURCES

# CONCLUSION

———

I still remember the day I pitched my two ideas for my book to Professor Eric Koester for his author program. The first one was a novel about purgatory in the form of a train (I still think it was a pretty cool idea—not sure if I could have followed through with it for a whole year though!) The second one, which I was honestly a lot less passionate about, was a book dedicated to the topic of Third Culture Kids. To my disappointment, Professor Koester found the TCK idea extremely interesting. He had never heard of the term before and thought it could have a positive impact on the world. Even as I was smiling at his enthusiastic reaction, I remember thinking in my head, *Ehhhh, I'm not too sure about that.*

Up until that point, I have never dedicated myself to actually studying the term Third Culture Kids. While I *knew* about the term already, I had never even spoken it out loud to anyone. I honestly wasn't sure how legitimate the term even was—whether it's even an actual word I'm allowed to use when describing myself to other people. I tried to look at this from the bright side.

*Well, I guess this makes it the perfect topic to write a book on.*

*Little* did I know, writers and creators have already crafted many scholarly works, books, TED Talks, and even short films about Third Culture Kids. I soon, in fact, realized that the problem wasn't the obscurity of the term TCK. It was finding a topic on TCKs that has not been discussed already (hence, why I decided to write on *teenage* TCKs).

Not only was writing *The Third Culture Teen* a learning experience for me, it truly was a journey of healing.

Only when I reached out to and interviewed other TCKs did I discover that I have actually been carrying a lot of insecurities in my heart.

Countless times, the interviews turned out to be more like my therapy sessions than actual "interviews." Conversations often divulged into me discussing my stories and my sweet interviewees listening to them and sharing their advice for me. It felt like learning to talk for the first time. Hearing older, wiser TCKs eloquently put the TCK experience into words taught me how to speak about my own TCK experience. I began to identify my insecurities and fears—of starting relationships, of leaving people behind, of belonging to a community. All these issues I thought I was alone in dealing with were actually universal experiences of hardship many TCKs could relate to. And that—knowing I wasn't alone in my suffering—was the most beautiful feeling anyone could ask for.

My hope is for this book to have at least half the impact all those amazing TCKs I have spoken with have had on me. I hope the book validated your pain, normalized your story, and encouraged you to go out and tell your own story to the world.

I hope to hear from you, readers, as well, and make more Third Culture Kid friends. I'm always open to more Third Culture Teen stories. Who knows? There might be enough to publish a part two! Please feel free to reach out to me about anything related to the TCK experience.

Thank you for reading!

March forward proudly and tell your story! We are the prototype of the human race in this rapidly globalizing world.

— Jiwon Lee,
February 24, 2020—my twenty-first birthday.
I officially grew out of being a TCT.

# ADDITIONAL RESOURCES

———

## ONLINE TCK COMMUNITIES

### 1. THIRD CULTURE KID GLOBAL (JAY THE TCK WEBSITE)
www.thirdculturekidglobal.com

Founded by "Jay the TCK," the website provides a community for TCKs and aims to connect Third Culture Kids across the world. It is associated with its own global Slack community, Instagram page, YouTube channel, Facebook group, and WhatsApp group. The WhatsApp group is very active and the Slack community (Citizens of the World) is fairly active as well.

I especially recommend the Slack community, which has different channels for various issues, such as mental health for TCKs, job networking between TCKs, a TCK musician channel, and more.

## 2. TCK WORLDWIDE

www.facebook.com/TCKWorldwide

TCK Worldwide is a Facebook page formed by Kristin Creekmore and Charlie Hancock that provides a "positive place to share and discuss all things relating to Third Culture Kids."[122]

## 3. TCK TOWN

www.tcktown.com

TCK TOWN is a monthly online journal presenting "candid, funny and profound stories by international writers."[123]

New articles are published on most Wednesdays and Saturdays. Alternatively, you can visit their website to sign up for their newsletter and receive a wrap up at the end of each month.[124]

## TCK ORGANIZATIONS & NONPROFITS

### 1. FAMILIES IN GLOBAL TRANSITION (FIGT)

www.figt.org

"Families in Global Transition is a welcoming forum for globally mobile individuals, families, and those working with them. We promote cross-sector connections for sharing

---

122 "Third Culture Kids (TCK)," TCK Worldwide, accessed April 25, 2020.

123 "TCK Town," TCK Town, accessed April 27, 2020.

124 Ibid.

research and developing best practices that support the growth, success and well-being of people crossing cultures around the world."[125]

An organization founded by Ruth Van Reken herself, it often hosts conferences and workshops for TCKs.

If you sign up for membership, $65 for individuals and $29 for students, you can have access to both online and offline resources in your country of residence, have contacts of other people around you who may be able to support you, and be included in an exclusive online community of other TCK members. They also have membership options for small businesses or international schools.[126]

Even without a membership, you can still access their free resources (including some of the workshops and conferences) or sign up for their newsletter.

## 2. TCKIDNOW
www.tckidnow.com

TCKid is a nonprofit organization that serves the community of ATCKs, ACCKs, and youth across geographical boundaries. It mostly acts as a social networking platform for its members.

---

125  "About FIGT," Families in Global Transition, accessed April 15, 2020.

126  Ibid.

Unlike the FIGT membership, joining the private social networking platform for TCKidNOW is free (although they do recommend an $8 donation/month).[127] The community has a membership of over twenty-three thousand people and includes local chapters around the world.[128]

They also provide TCK research funding and produce TV/radio content related to TCK life.

### 3. BRATS WITHOUT BORDERS
www.bratswithoutborders.org

Brats Without Borders is a nonprofit owned by filmmaker Donna Musil mostly supporting US military brats, but also TCKs in general.

They hold workshops for schools and have an internal art institute to provide art camps and art workshops for military brat TCKs interested in art. The nonprofit also has its own Facebook group (www.facebook.com/groups/bratswithoutborders) consisting mostly of American military brats.

### 4. INTERACTION INTERNATIONAL
www.interactionintl.org

Interaction International is an organization based in the United States with the mission of providing a "flow of care

---

127  "About: Vision and Mission," TCKidNow, accessed April 20, 2020.

128  Ibid.

for the global TCK community."[129] They hold seminars for TCKs of different age groups, ranging from younger teens to adults looking for jobs. Their website also has free resources and magazines for TCKs to reference.

## TCK BOOKS

### 1. *THIRD CULTURE KIDS: GROWING UP AMONGST WORLDS* BY RUTH VAN REKEN, DAVID C. POLLOCK, AND MICHAEL V. POLLOCK

The ultimate "bible" on TCKs. With three editions total, the 2010 version is the most recent book.

Authors David Pollock (the latest version is also coauthored by his son, Michael Pollock) and Ruth Van Reken are the pioneers of the TCK profile, and hence, the book provides a very comprehensive view on not only TCKs but ATCKs and CCKs as well.

It's a bit technical in the beginning, but the latter part includes more personal writings and interviews.

### 2. *FINDING HOME: THIRD CULTURE KIDS IN THE WORLD* BY RACHEL PIEH JONES

*Finding Home: Third Culture Kids in the World* is a collection of essays written by various TCKs. The essays, some of which are written by the author herself, are divided into

---

129 "Our Vision & Mission," Interaction International, accessed April 28, 2020.

different chapters/topics such as "Parenting Third Culture Kids" or "Thriving as Third Culture Kids." All the essays are beautifully written and feature authors from various backgrounds, ranging from Rachel who is a mother of a TCK child to young TCTs to professionals who are experts on Third Culture Kids psychology.

### 3. *MISUNDERSTOOD: THE IMPACT OF GROWING UP OVERSEAS IN THE 21ST CENTURY* BY TANYA CROSSMAN

Tanya Crossman is another author whose expertise is TCKs and their lifestyle. The book is divided into sections for specific situations an ATCK might be in and focuses on practical support methods based on research and anecdotes from various TCKs.

### 4. *THE GLOBAL NOMAD'S GUIDE TO UNIVERSITY TRANSITION* BY TINA QUICK

Tina Quick is an ATCK who raised three TCK daughters. She is currently a cross-cultural trainer and international speaker who works with international schools all over the world. Her book provides practical suggestions specifically for TCTs who are transitioning to college. It also includes anecdotes from other TCTs who have successfully adjusted to college. If you are going to be moving to college soon, I strongly recommend this book as a guide before your big transition.

## TCK MAGAZINES

### 1. DENIZEN MAGAZINE
www.denizenmag.com

*Denizen* is an online magazine dedicated to Third Culture Kids. It represents the "modern global nomad community, complete with attitude, expression and creativity."[130] While not updated today, you can still find interesting archived articles written by different TCKs. Steph Yiu's story from Chapter 9 is an article from this magazine.

### 2. AMONG WORLDS MAGAZINE
www.interactionintl.org/publications/among-worlds-magazine

*Among Worlds* publishes both physical and digital magazines about ATCK issues with relationships, grief, transitions, home, values, and many more. "Each edition tackles a specific issue that is relevant to ATCKs in a head-on approach."[131] You can order each edition for $4.99.

---

130  "About," Denizen Magazine, accessed April 16, 2020.

131  "Among Worlds Magazine," Interaction International, accessed April 30, 2020.

# ACKNOWLEDGMENTS

First and foremost, I'd like to thank my parents and my sister who literally began the TCK journey with me back when I was eight years old and stayed with me through it, all the way to present day. I have had times when I blamed my parents for the constant transitions, yet, today, finishing up this book on Third Culture Teens, I can now confidently say having lived across the world was a true blessing for me.

I'd like to give a big thank you to everyone at New Degree Press for making this book come to life. Without you guys— Professor Koester, Brian, Melody, Cynthia, fellow authors, and other staff—this book could not have come to life.

I'd also like to sincerely thank all the interviewees who took time out of their busy schedules to tell their amazing stories to me: Lindie, Jessica, Rachel, Kayla, Amy, Fareeha, Ruth, Kawtar, Grace, DaeYoung, and Isabelle! This book would have been nothing without your kindness and courage to share your story with me. I especially want to thank Kawtar for introducing me to other cool ATCKs and continuing to help me revise and promote the book even after the interview.

I also want to, again, thank Ruth Van Reken for giving me the encouragement I needed to make it through the rest of the revision process. Thank you so very much. Each and every one of you are my role models, and I know your stories will inspire other TCT readers just as they have inspired me!

An equally warm thank you to all my beta-readers/supporters of *The Third Culture Teen*—listed in alphabetical order below:

Arnao, Sophia
Baek, Gena
Botes, Lindie
Cahill, Fiona
Carr, Christa
Chang, Sinead
Chinamanthur, Niki
Chiong, Marco
Choi, Eun Seo
Chow, Sarah
Connally, Meghan
Dureg, Clarence
Eim, Sarah
El Alaoui, Kawtar
Hadiwijoyo, Jessica
Harianto, Natasha
Jenkins, Abby
Kang, Hyunsook
Kang, Min ju
Kang, Yee Sun
Keum, Eunyoung
Ki, Mijung
Kim, Abigail

Kim, Ae Jung
Kim, Ahhyun
Kim, Dae Hyun
Kim, HyoJeon
Kim, James
Kim, Jessica Minsol
Kim, Joo Young
Kim, Sangchul
Kobayashi, Tamaki
Koester, Eric
Koo, Jean-Mo
Kosinac, Nadina
Kwon, Kyoungja
Lee, Christine
Lee, Grace
Lee, Gun Woo
Lee, Hyunsoo
Lee, Jaejin
Lee, Jihyun
Lee, Jocelyn
Lee, Jooho
Lee, Moonhee
Lee, Okseon

Lee, Wonyoung
Lee, Youn
Lee, Young Ju
Lei, Xinya
Lin, Michelle
Locke, Dylan J.
Mahmood, Fareeha
Mandi, Natasha
McCown, Star
McMillen, Amy
Min, Jenny
Minematsu, Aiko
Moon, Christy
Navidad, Patricia M.
Park, Cindy
Park, Sung Jong
Park, Young Joo
Patrouillard, Quentin
Pham, Aaron
Reken, Ruth Van

S I
Salinas, Christian
Scott,Carolyn
Seo, Eunjung
Seo, Hyuk Su
Seo, Jeongju
Seo, Sang-wook
Son, Miriam
Son, Sung Hye
Song, Ji-Hye
Song, Jing
Takahashi, Danielle
Teusink, Rebekah
Wang, Jerry
Wang, Ji Hun
Wang, Linye
Whykatherine,
Yang, Angela
Yang, Gary
Zhao, Xinyu (Ciao)

Thank you for believing in our cause to normalize the TCK experience.

I would also like to recognize everyone else who is not mentioned above for all their help in promoting the book and being there for me throughout the writing process. Thank you for making this book a reality!

# APPENDIX

—

## INTRODUCTION

The Editors of Encyclopaedia Britannica. "Audrey Hepburn." In *Encyclopædia Britannica. Encyclopædia Britannica, inc. 2020.* https://www.britannica.com/biography/Audrey-Hepburn.

The Editors of Encyclopaedia Britannica. "Freddie Mercury." In *Encyclopædia Britannica. Encyclopædia Britannica, inc. 2020.* https://www.britannica.com/biography/Freddie-Mercury.

Pollock, David C., Ruth E. Van Reken, and Michael V. Pollock. *Third Culture Kids: Growing Up Among Worlds.* Boston: Nicholas Brealey Publishing, 2010.

Wallenfeldt, Jeff, and David Mendell. "Barack Obama." In *Encyclopædia Britannica. Encyclopædia Britannica, inc. 2020.* https://www.britannica.com/biography/Barack-Obama#ref281896.

## CHAPTER 1

Long, Daniel. "Asian Third Culture Kids: A Phenomenological Study of the Cross-Cultural Identity of Chinese Students Educated in a Western-Curriculum International School." Doctoral thesis, Northeastern University, 2016.

Pollock, David C., Ruth E. Van Reken, and Michael V. Pollock. *Third Culture Kids: Growing Up Among Worlds.* Boston: Nicholas Brealey Publishing, 2010.

## CHAPTER 2

Packard, Erika. "That teenage feeling: Harvard researchers may have found biological clues to quirky adolescent behavior." *American Psychological Association* 38, no. 4 (2007). https://www.apa.org/monitor/apr07/teenage

## CHAPTER 3

*New Oxford English Dictionary,* 2nd ed, s.v. "Home."

Schuilenberg, Susannah-Joy. "A Whole Self." In *Finding Home: Third Culture Kids in the World,* edited by Rachel Pieh Jones (Washington: Amazon), 2018.

## CHAPTER 5

Desjarlais, Malinda and Jessica J. Joseph. "Socially Interactive and Passive Technologies Enhance Friendship Quality: An Investigation of the Mediating Roles of Online and Offline Self-Disclosure." *Cyberpsychology, Behavior, and Social Networking* 20, no. 5 (2017).

Valencia, Erika. "Neo-Filipino: A Study on the Impact of Internet and Mobile Technology on the Identity of Selected Filipino Third Culture Kids." Master's thesis, University of Santo Tomas, 2016.

Young, Kimberly S. and Robert C. Rogers. "The Relationship Between Depression and Internet Addiction." *Cyberpsychology & Behavior* 1, no. 1 (1998).

## CHAPTER 6

"Older Teens." Interaction International. Accessed April 3, 2020. https://interactionintl.org/programs/transition-seminar/older-teens/

Oxford, "Definition of adulting in English." LEXICO powered by Oxord. Accessed 21 February 2020. https://www.lexico.com/en/definition/adulting.

Purnell, Laura, and Elizabeth Hoban. "The lived experiences of Third Culture Kids transitioning into university life in Australia." *International Journal of Intercultural Relations* 41 (2014).

## CHAPTER 8

Mayberry, Kate. "Third Culture Kids: Citizens of everywhere and nowhere." *BBC,* November 19, 2016. https://www.bbc.com/worklife/article/20161117-third-culture-kids-citizens-of-everywhere-and-nowhere

Pollock, David C., Ruth E. Van Reken, and Michael V. Pollock. *Third Culture Kids: Growing Up Among Worlds.* Boston: Nicholas Brealey Publishing, 2010.

Shen-Berro, Julian and Kimmy Yan. "As Coronavirus Spreads, so does Concern over Xenophobia." NBC News, January 29, 2020, https://www.nbcnews.com/news/Asian-america/coronavirus-spreads-so-does-concern-over-xenophobia-n1125441

Tanu, Danau. "Global Nomads: Towards a Study of 'Asian' Third Culture Kids." *Conference: 17th Biennial Conference of the Asian Studies Association of Australia, At Melbourne* (2008).

## CHAPTER 9

Schubert, Esther. "Keeping Third-Culture Kids Emotionally Healthy: Depression and Suicide Among Missionary Kids." in *ICMK Compendium: New Directions for Mission: Implications for MK,* edited by Beth A. Tetzel and Patricia Mortenson. Brattleboro: Association of Christian Schools International, 1986.

"Third Culture Kids/Global Nomands." Lewis & Clark College. accessed March 27, 2020. https://www.lclark.edu/offices/international/third_culture_kids/

Yiu, Steph. "Not 'coming home' alone." Denizen for third culture kids, December 6, 2008. https://denizenmag.com/2008/12/not-coming-home-alone/?fbclid=IwAR3iWARV7XKRT-1kAWnHOXWNAzkNwU715AXT8tiJmTQvnVXHT6d1X-VcKZPdg

## CHAPTER 10

Dewaele, Jean-Marc and Jan Pieter van Oudenhoven. "The effect of multilingualism/multiculturalism on personality: no gain without pain for Third Culture Kids?" *International Journal of Multilingualism* 6, no. 4 (2009).

Melles, Elizabeth A. and Jonathan Schwartz. "Does the third culture kid experience predict level of prejudice?" *International Journal of Intercultural Relations* 37, no. 2 (2013).

Straffon, David A. "Assessing the intercultural sensitivity of high school students attending an international school." *International Journal of Intercultural Relations* 27, no. 4 (2003).

Vyhmeister, Erik. "Building Identity as a Third Culture Kid | Erik Vyhmeister | TEDxAndrewsUniversity." TEDx Talks, May 26, 2015, video. https://www.youtube.com/watch?v=8RCmgMK-JRy8.

## CHAPTER 12

Bytter, Morgan. "Career Choices and the Influence of Third Culture Kids on International Relations." Undergraduate honors thesis, University of Arkansas, Fayetteville, 2012.

Cottrell, Ann Baker and Ruth Hill Useem. "TCKs Four Times More Likely to Earn Bachelor's Degrees." *TCK World: The Official Home of Third Culture Kids,* April 11, 2009. http://www.tckworld.com/useem/art2.html.

"Freddie Mercury's complex relationship with Zanzibar." *BBC*, October 23, 2018. https://www.bbc.com/news/world-africa-45900712

*Inside Edition.* "Inside the Home Where Obama Grew Up in Indonesia." August 13, 2019. Video. https://www.youtube.com/watch?v=O1-MF6qfJ8k&t=2s

*Lindie Botes.* "Joys and challenges of being a Third Culture Kid | Where is home?" April 16, 2018. Video. https://www.youtube.com/watch?v=vwqo627nMpc&t=78s

Mason, Margie. "Obama pushes tolerance, respect in childhood home, Jakarta." *Washington Post*, July 2, 2017.

Obama, Barack. *Dreams From My Father.* New York: Three Rivers Press, 2004.

Suh, WonSeop. "Surprise TCK: Freddie Mercury." *Cultures: The Global Multicultural Magazine,* May 1, 2014. https://cultursmag.com/freddie-mercury/.

## CHAPTER 13

"About," Ema Ryan Yamazaki, accessed April 1, 2020. http://www.emaexplorations.com/about

"About, " Road Home Film, accessed April 1, 2020. https://roadhomefilm.com/enjoy-the-road-home.html

Bouraoui, Nina. *Tomboy.* Lincoln: U of Nebraska Press, 2007.

Brats Without Borders, Inc. "About the Film." *Brats: Our Journey Home,* Accessed April 1, 2020. http://www.bratsourjourney-home.com/about.htm

Brats Without Borders, Inc. "Filmmaker." *Brats: Our Journey Home,* accessed April 1, 2020. http://www.bratsourjourney-home.com/filmmakers.htm

Brats Without Borders, Inc. "The Nonprofit." *Brats: Our Journey Home,* Accessed April 1, 2020. http://www.bratsourjourney-home.com/about.htm

Damlé, Amaleena. "Nina Bouraoui." Institute of Modern Language Research. accessed April 1, 2020. https://modernlanguages.sas.ac.uk/research-centres/centre-study-contemporary-womens-writing/languages/french/nina-bouraoui

"Director," Road Home Film, accessed April 1, 2020. https://road-homefilm.com/Rahul-gandotra.html

Haikaa. "Work of Art." By Haikaa. Track 1 on *Work of Art.* Haikaa Music, YouTube.

Jones, Shelley. "Does a Nomadic Childhood Lead to a More Creative Life? Uprooted Kids." Huck Magazine, July 22, 2015, http://www.huckmagazine.com/art-and-culture/uprooted-kids/

Larkin, Colin. *The Virgin Encyclopedia of Popular Music.* London: Virgin Books, 1997.

Rauwerda, Antje M., "Expatriate Versus Third Culture (Chris Pavone Vs. Belinda Bauer)." *Third Culture Literature* (blog),

March 21, 2017. https://thirdcultureliterature.blogspot. com/2017/03/expatriate-versus-third-culture-chris.html

Sanfilippo-Schulz, Jessica. "Escaping National Tags and Embracing Diversity: Third Culture Kid Songwriters." *Open Cultural Studies* 2 (2018).

"Sinkane," BBC Music, BBC, accessed April 1, 2020. https://www.bbc.co.uk/music/artists/b15d17d4-37ea-4410-9ae4-60b5eee03459

Tikaram, Tanita. "My Enemy." By Matt Radford and Tanita Tikaram. Track 10 on *Closer to the People*. Ear Music, compact disc.

Yamamoto, Haikaa. *What Is Diversity?: A Work of Art to Celebrate a Diverse World* Scotts Valley: CreateSpace Independent Pub, 2012.

## ADDITIONAL RESOURCES

"About." Denizen Magazine. Accessed April 16, 2020. https://denizenmag.com/about/

"About FIGT." Families in Global Transition. Accessed April 15, 2020. https://figt.org/About_FIGT

"About: Vision and Mission." TCKidNow. Accessed April 20, 2020. https://www.tckidnow.com/about/vision-mission/

"Among Worlds Magazine." Interaction International. Accessed April 30, 2020. https://interactionintl.org/PUBLICATIONS/ AMONG-WORLDS-MAGAZINE/

"Our Vision & Mission." Interaction International. Accessed April 28, 2020. https://interactionintl.org/about-us/our-mission-vision/

"Third Culture Kids (TCK)." TCK Worldwide. Accessed April 25, 2020. https://www.facebook.com/pg/TCKWorldwide/about/?ref=page_internal

"TCK Town." TCK Town. Accessed April 27, 2020. https://www.facebook.com/pg/tcktown/about/?

Printed by Amazon Italia Logistica S.r.l.
Torrazza Piemonte (TO), Italy

53059921R00132